First World War
and Army of Occupation
War Diary
France, Belgium and Germany

41 DIVISION
Divisional Troops
Royal Army Medical Corps
139 Field Ambulance
21 April 1916 - 31 October 1917

WO95/2629/1

The Naval & Military Press Ltd
www.nmarchive.com
Published in association with The National Archives

Published by

The Naval & Military Press Ltd

Unit 10 Ridgewood Industrial Park,
Uckfield, East Sussex,
TN22 5QE England
Tel: +44 (0) 1825 749494

www.naval-military-press.com
www.nmarchive.com

This diary has been reprinted in facsimile from the original. Any imperfections are inevitably reproduced and the quality may fall short of modern type and cartographic standards.

© **Crown Copyright**
Images reproduced by permission of The National Archives, London, England, 2015.

Contents

Document type	Place/Title	Date From	Date To
Heading	WO95/2629-1		
Heading	41st Division 139th Fld Ambulance May 1916-Oct 1917 Mar 1918-1919 Oct Italy 1917 Nov 1918 Feb		
Heading	41st Div 139th F. Amb. End of April 1916 May 1916		
Miscellaneous	From O.C. 139th Field Ambulance	02/06/1916	02/06/1916
War Diary	Haig Hutments	21/04/1916	03/05/1916
War Diary	Havre	04/05/1916	05/05/1916
War Diary	Godewaers-Velde Caestre	06/05/1916	06/05/1916
War Diary	Rouge Croix	07/05/1916	08/05/1916
War Diary	Strazelle	09/05/1916	15/05/1916
War Diary	Caestre	16/05/1916	29/05/1916
War Diary	Bailleul	30/05/1916	31/05/1916
Miscellaneous	From O.C. 139th Field Ambulance.	03/07/1916	03/07/1916
War Diary	D.R.S. Bailleul	01/06/1916	04/06/1916
War Diary	Bailleul	04/06/1916	30/06/1916
Heading	War Diary 139th Field Ambulance Volume III July 1916		
War Diary	Bailleul	01/07/1916	31/07/1916
Heading	War Diary of 139th Field Amb Augt 1st 1916 to Augt 31st 1916 Volume 4		
War Diary	Bailleul	01/08/1916	18/08/1916
War Diary	27 X.1.b.3.3	19/08/1916	19/08/1916
War Diary	27.X16.3.3 Bailleul	19/08/1916	23/08/1916
War Diary	B Train	24/08/1916	24/08/1916
War Diary	Longpres	24/08/1916	24/08/1916
War Diary	Ergnies	25/08/1916	31/08/1916
Heading	War Diary of 139th Fld Amb. 41st Division From 1/9/16 to 30/9/16 (Volume V.)		
War Diary	Ergnies	01/09/1916	04/09/1916
War Diary	Becordel	05/09/1916	28/09/1916
War Diary	Shrine & Quarry.	29/09/1916	01/10/1916
Heading	War Diary 139th Field Amb. October 1916 Vol 6		
War Diary		01/10/1916	14/10/1916
War Diary	Dernancourt.	15/10/1916	18/10/1916
War Diary	Wanel	19/10/1916	31/10/1916
Heading	41 Div. War Diary of 139th Field Ambulance November 1916 Volume VII		
War Diary		01/11/1916	30/11/1916
Miscellaneous			
Heading	41st Div. War Diary of 139th Field Ambulance From Dec. 1st 16 to Dec 31st 16 Volume VIII		
War Diary		01/12/1916	08/12/1916
War Diary	Sheet 28 N 7b 1.4	09/12/1916	31/12/1916
Heading	41st Div. War Diary 139th Field Ambulance From Jan 1st 1917 To Jan 31st 1917 Volume 9		
War Diary	N 7 C 3.5 Sheet 28	01/01/1917	31/01/1917
Heading	41st Div War Diary 139th Field Ambulance From 1/2/17 To 2/2/17 Vol 10		
War Diary	Sheet 28 N 7 C h.3.1	01/02/1917	17/02/1917
War Diary	N 7 C 4.3	18/02/1917	24/02/1917

Type	Description	Date From	Date To
War Diary	N 7 C 4.3 Sheet 28 Belgium	25/02/1917	28/02/1917
Operation(al) Order(s)	Medical Arrangements by O.C. 139th Field Ambulance in connection with 124th Infantry Brigade Order No 95. Appendix I	22/02/1917	22/02/1917
Map			
Miscellaneous	Report on the arrangements made for the evacuation of wounded in connection with Operations by 124th Infantry Brigade on the night of Feb 24/25 1917. Appendix II	24/02/1917	24/02/1917
Diagram etc	Main Dressing Station. Plan of Arrangements For The Night Of February 24th & 25th 1917		
Heading	41st Div War Diary 139th Field Ambulance From 1st March 1917 To 31st March 1917 Vol XI		
War Diary	N 7 Ch. 3 Sheet 28 Belgium 1-40,000	01/03/1917	21/03/1917
War Diary	Sheet 27 NE 1-20,000 K 31,C, 2.1.	22/03/1917	31/03/1917
Heading	War Diary 139th Field Ambulance R.A.M.C. From 1st April 1917 To 30th April 1917 Vol 12		
War Diary	Steenvorde	01/04/1917	06/04/1917
War Diary	Sheet 27 N.E. Belgium 1-20,000 428 d 5.5	07/04/1917	30/04/1917
Operation(al) Order(s)	139th Field Ambulance R.A.M.C. Operation Order No 2. Appendix 1	04/04/1917	04/04/1917
Miscellaneous	Orders For Advanced Warning Party. Appendix 2	30/04/1917	30/04/1917
Miscellaneous	Orders For Advanced Party. Appendix 3	04/04/1917	04/04/1917
Heading	War Diary 139th Field Ambulance R.A.M.C. From 1st May 1917 To 31st May 1917 Vol 13		
War Diary	41st D.R.S Wippenhoek	01/05/1917	14/05/1917
War Diary	Sheet 27 NE L 28b. 7.7	15/05/1917	31/05/1917
Heading	War Diary 139th Field Ambulance R.A.M.C. From 1/6/17 to 30/6/17 Vol 14		
Miscellaneous	Plan of D.R.S.		
Miscellaneous			
War Diary	Sheet NE (b) 4. 28b. 7.7	01/06/1917	01/06/1917
War Diary	Sheet 27 N.E, b 428. b.6.7	02/06/1917	06/06/1917
War Diary	Sheet 27 NE 428, d, 3.6	06/06/1917	14/06/1917
War Diary	Sheet 27 R 10.a. 3.3	15/06/1917	27/06/1917
War Diary	Sheet 27 S.E. R. 10,a. 4.7	28/06/1917	30/06/1917
Operation(al) Order(s)	139th Field Ambulance Operation Order No. 3 Appendix 1	06/06/1917	06/06/1917
Operation(al) Order(s)	Operation Order No. 4. Appendix 3	12/06/1917	12/06/1917
Heading	War Diary 139th Field Ambulance R.A.M.C. From 1st July 1917 To 31st July 1917 Vol 15		
War Diary	R 10 a 3.3. Sheet 27 S.E.	01/07/1917	25/07/1917
War Diary	Vormozeele	26/07/1917	30/07/1917
War Diary	Belgium Sheet 28 N W I 31 C 3.4.	31/07/1917	31/07/1917
Heading	War Diary 139th Field Ambulance R.A.M.C. From 1st August 1917 To 31st August 1917 Vol 16		
War Diary	I.31 C 3.4 Map Zillebeke Belgium Sheet 28 N.W.	01/08/1917	01/08/1917
War Diary	I 31, C,3,4 Ref Zillebeke	01/08/1917	02/08/1917
War Diary	I 31,C, 3.4	03/08/1917	13/08/1917
War Diary	I 31 C, 3.4 Map Zillebeke Belgium Sheet 28 N.W.	14/08/1917	14/08/1917
War Diary	Sheet 27 S.E (B. Series) X 2b 2.3	15/08/1917	20/08/1917
War Diary	Staples	20/08/1917	21/08/1917
War Diary	Sheet 36d NE F 1 C 3.5	21/08/1917	31/08/1917
Map	139th Field Ambulance R.A.M.C.		
Operation(al) Order(s)	Operation Order No. 5. 139th Field Ambulance. Copy No. 1	26/07/1917	26/07/1917

Miscellaneous	Appendix "A".		
Heading	War Diary of 139 Field Ambulance Sept 1st 1917 to Sept 30th 1917 Volume II		
War Diary	Sheet 36d N E	01/09/1917	04/09/1917
War Diary	Sheet 36d N F 31d 3.3	05/09/1917	11/09/1917
War Diary	La Clytte	11/09/1917	23/09/1917
War Diary	Hondeghe Sheet 27 SE V 3 b 3.7	24/09/1917	25/09/1917
War Diary	Sheet 27 SE V 3b 3.7 Sheet 19	26/09/1917	27/09/1917
War Diary	L 29 C 22 Sheet 19 D 9 C 3.7	27/09/1917	28/09/1917
War Diary	Sheet 19 D 9 C. 3.7	29/09/1917	30/09/1917
Heading	War Diary 139th Field Ambulance R.A.M.C. October 1917 Volume 2		
War Diary	Sheet 19 D9c 3.7	01/10/1917	07/10/1917
War Diary	Sheet 11SE W 10 C 7.7	07/10/1917	14/10/1917
War Diary	Sheet 19 D8 a 2.6	15/10/1917	16/10/1917
War Diary	D8a 2.6	17/10/1917	25/10/1917
War Diary	D8a 7.6	26/10/1917	29/10/1917
War Diary	La Panne	30/10/1917	31/10/1917
Miscellaneous	Appendix 1		
Operation(al) Order(s)	Routine Orders No. 223 By Lieut. Col. G.G. Collet, R.A.M.C. Commanding "B" Field Ambulance, R.A.M.C. 1st September 1918	01/09/1918	01/09/1918
Miscellaneous	A.D.M.S. 41st. Division.	09/08/1918	09/08/1918

WD 95 / 2629 (1929)

WD 95 / 2630 (1929)

41ST DIVISION

139TH FLD AMBULANCE

MAY 1916 - ~~DEC 1916~~ OCT 1917
MAR 1918 — 1919 OCT

End of April 1914
May 1916

S/ 9th of April

139 F. Amb.

Dec. 18

COMMITTEE FOR THE
MEDICAL HISTORY OF THE WAR
Date 26 JUN 1915

Secret

From
O.C.
139 1/2 Field Ambulance

To
Officer i/c
Q.g. Office
Base Rouen –

Herewith my War Diary
from the first day of
Mobilization April 21st 1916
to May 31st 1916.

A.W. Long Major
RAMC.
O.C. 139 1/2 Field
Ambulance

June 2nd
1916.

139 F Amb
Vol 1

VOLUME I
SECRET No I.
Army Form C. 2118

APRIL 1916

WAR DIARY or INTELLIGENCE SUMMARY
139 (1st) Field Ambulance
April 21st - May 21st 1916

(Erase heading not required.)

Instructions regarding War Diaries and Intelligence Summaries are contained in F.S. Regs., Part II. and the Staff Manual respectively. Title Pages will be prepared in manuscript.

Place	Date	Hour	Summary of Events and Information	Remarks and references to Appendices
HAIG HUTMENTS	21.4.16		Received orders to join Division	A.J.& L.
"	22.4.16		Special instruction in trench warfare yesterday + today.	App. 15.
"	23.4.16		Church Parade -	App. 15.
"	24.4.16		Packing of wagons and general preparation	App.
"	25.4.16		Rehearsal for King's Inspection	App.
"	26.4.16		King's Inspection of Division.	App.
"	27.4.16		Divisional Route march only 2 of our unit fell out.	App.
"	28.4.16		Rest day -	App.
"	29.4.16		Camp fatigues. Church Parade -	App.
"	30.4.16			App.
"	31.4.16		Packing of wagons, and general preparation for a move.	

Jas. Long, Major R.A.M.C.
O.C. 139/1st Field Ambulance.

WAR DIARY or INTELLIGENCE SUMMARY

Army Form C. 2118

VOLUME II No II

MAY 1916

Place	Date	Hour	Summary of Events and Information	Remarks and references to Appendices
HAIG HUTMENTS	1-5-16		Rest day —	Hart. Gpt.
"	2.5.16		Medical inspection of units & Kensing over of Barracks.	Hart. Gpt.
"	3.5.16	3-15 AM	Entrained at Farnborough for Southampton and Embarked at 4-30 p.m.	Hart. Gpt.
HAVRE	4-5-16	10-30 AM	Disembarked at HAVRE and arrived at No 2 Rest Camp at 6-30 p.m.	Hart. Gpt.
HAVRE	5.5.16	8 p.m.	Entrained at HAVRE - Point 6. Sent one NCO to No 9 Stationary Hospital Havre.	Gpt.
GODEWAERS- VELDE	6.5.16		Arrived at GODEWAERSVELDE 11-30 p.m.	Gpt.
CAESTRE			Paraded for the night & went into billets at ROUGE CROIX being accomm. at Boetel in La Ferme Vig. M-Lealott d'esqélie & M-Jules R-9-8 ast.	
ROUGE CROIX	7-5-16		Inspecting Billets & cesses admitted & inoculated to D.D.S. at STRAZEELE.	Gpt.
"	8.5.16		Inspecting Billets. Y.A. given a practical instruction in sanitation by ye Chemical advises. Remarks on Billets. Horse accommodation for men fair. No proper accommodation for Officers. Horse lines for 0. Waterguft for drinking. Sanitation of farm bad. The manure middens unfit for the water supply. The Sanitary police to be obtained from CAESTRE.	
STRAZELLE	9.5.16		Took over duties at Amb. Rcvg. from 13/3 F.A. and 12 patients and permitted later. Myches from A.D.M.S. 2nd Army held and to officers of this unit proceeded to A.D.M.S. 19 Divn. H.Q. ARMENTIERES and 2/15 F.A. STEENWARCK for instructional purposes. Lieut Q. Rottemann detailed to proceed to 189 - Inf. Batt. R.A.C. for temporary duty by order from A.D.M.S.	Gpt.

No III

Army Form C. 2118

WAR DIARY
or
INTELLIGENCE SUMMARY

(Erase heading not required.)

MAY 1916

Place	Date	Hour	Summary of Events and Information	Remarks and references to Appendices
	9.5.16		Comparing Ridlet's the semi nominates appears to me Ridlet's as to items mentioned in lists 8 & 12 not. Except that NCC walks is Qr for messing tea, and that have been employed in that matter.	
STRAZEELE	10.5.16		Patients admitted 13. Discharged 11 to No.12 C.C.S. HAZEBROUCK.	
"	11.5.16		Patients admitted 4. Discharged 3. Our motor Ambulance & motor bicycle arrived today.	
"	12.5.16		Myself + 1st & 4 officers returned today from course of instruction and divr. Sheldon Emery + Todd sent to A.D.M.S. 1st for instruction under A.D.M.S. Patients admitted 15. Discharged 4. Applied to R.E. 41 Div. for pumps to empty used lodging to this station which is very bad —	
"	13.5.16		Patients admitted 12. Discharged 9. Received search orders for exchange area.	
"	14.5.16		Church parade at Strazeele. Received orders to get two more field ambulances from A.D.M.S. — Viz 139th Y.A. to take over from the 57 F.A. at CAESTRE.	
"	15.5.16		Lieut. D.P. Thomas has proceeded to BAILLEUL for welfare arrangements for two weeks. Lieut Empey with advanced party proceeded to CAESTRE.	

Army Form C. 2118 — No IV.

WAR DIARY or INTELLIGENCE SUMMARY

(Erase heading not required.)

MAY 1916

Place	Date	Hour	Summary of Events and Information	Remarks and references to Appendices
CAESTRE	16/5/16		The 139 F.A. taken over from the 52nd F.d. Ambulance at CAESTRE. Lieut. W. Wilson R.A.M.C. proceeded to its 9th Entrenching Battalion for duty in order from O/C A.D.M.S. Lieut A.J. Cluering went with 5 NCO and 11 men (proceeded to D.R.S. at BAILLEUL) from an situational purposes according to orders from the A.D.M.S.	recd.
"	17/5/16		The day spent in cleaning out, and rearranging the whole a.R.S. with the R.A.M.C. Personnel are placed in tents. One officer detailed as visiting officer for the week + one present orderly one " " Surgical " " + one surgical dresser one " " Medical " " + one sergt., Nurse one " " Orderly " " " " The orderly officer every to at any time one to the above + one weekly orderly sgt. one Sergeant detailed as Receiving Sergeant + one PG assistant one " " Dispenser " + one PG assistant one Corporal " Pack Store Cpl. + one PG assistant one Sergeant " for A + D. Book and one same Cpl. one Corporal " Bath Room one " " as Chiropodist & 3 PG assistants one " " as Chiropodist & their writer + one assistant	Sd.

WAR DIARY or INTELLIGENCE SUMMARY

Army Form C. 2118

No V.

MAY 1916

Place	Date	Hour	Summary of Events and Information	Remarks and references to Appendices
			One corporal detailed for Sanitary duties with 4 assistants	
			One special P.C. detailed for incinerator with one assistant.	
			One sergeant detailed for Drawing Rations with one assistant.	
			One Q.M. Sergt.	
			One sergeant } detailed for Q-M. Stores with two assistants.	
			One corporal	
			Lieut. O'Neill Graffey died of Embolism due to Cerebral Meningitis.	Hw
CAESTRE	15.5.16		A count of enquiry held also a P.M. on Lieut Graffey this morning when the above result was discovered. He is burned took place in the evening. The army Service Corps forming a firing party. A message from the A.D.M.S. ordering one section to be ready at short notice to act under orders from the O.C. 124 Infantry Brigade. Section C. has been detailed under the command of Lieut. Corkill	
			One Lance Corporal detailed as shoe maker and one assistant	
			One Female Sergeant detailed as carpenter and one assistant	
			One Private detailed as Tin Smith and one assistant	Hw

WAR DIARY or INTELLIGENCE SUMMARY

Army Form C. 2118

MAY 1916

Place	Date	Hour	Summary of Events and Information	Remarks and references to Appendices
CAESTRE	19.5.16		Lieut. Childing-Smith has returned from Walts. Reconnaissance. All sickies to be sent to 50 C.C.S. via 1st 9/12 Divn R.S. BAILLEUL by abbon from the 2 A.M.S. The patients are divided daily into (a) Those rejoining their units (b) Those for C.C.S. (c) Those for retention. In retention of evacuation to MONT-DES-CATS. The A.D.M.S. is only to admit cases likely to be well within 7 days and those under treatment of any one time should not exceed 200. Those who have not recovered in 14 days must be either (a) evacuated to C.C.S. (b) If likely to be fit to return to duty within a further period of 7 days sent to Mont-des-Cats.	Ans.
"	20-5-16		I have reported to the War Office w/e of 9th A.D.M.S. the death of Lieut. H. Moffat, and applied for a man to fill his place.	Ans
"	21-5-16		Parade Service at 10-30. Evening Service 6-30 pm & 7-30 pm. The 192 patients taken over on the 16/12 from this Division 1/ Division have all been evacuated. Leave 21.	Ans
"	22.5.16		The patients are encouraged to play football & properly considered fit, by a medical officer.	Ans

No VII.

Army Form C. 2118

WAR DIARY
or
INTELLIGENCE SUMMARY
(Erase heading not required.)

MAY 1916

Place	Date	Hour	Summary of Events and Information	Remarks and references to Appendices
CAESTRE	22.5.16		Our D.R.S. was Inspected today by the D.D.M.S. II Corps Colonel R.G.A. Gibbes - and Colonel Elliot A.D.M.S. 41st Division. He recommended the Italian stove in the Chateau, and the Well in the Compound to be put in working order. In reply to Information asked for by the A in C. as to the desire of men to get settlement of employment on the Land, after the War, the following has been the result on enquiry N.T. No asked 244 Yes 34 No against 210. Nearly all those also furnish would on the land, some would for Long. — New D.R.T. Ronnia returned for duty.	fwd
"	23/5/16		Separate A.T. A. 36 are kept for N.Midl Canadian, Australian & N.Zealand eve. It has been found that the divisionization of blankets with the MTS is to the half on hour is not sufficient. I shall keep 2 Railins on for 1/2 an hour in e. 40, to call solution.	fwd
"	24/5/16		All our Officers have seen the working of Regimental ambical units. Advanced dressing Stations from D.S. C.C. S & D.R.S. as well as the Rest Station in use in each area. Surgeon general R. Porter, D.M.S. Second Army accompanied by Colonel Godsay Inspected our D.R.S. and took much Interest in the arrangements.	fwd

1875 Wt. W593/826 1,000,000 4/15 J.B.C. & A. A.D.S.S./Forms/C. 2118.

No VIII

WAR DIARY
or
INTELLIGENCE SUMMARY

Army Form C. 2118

MAY 1916

Place	Date	Hour	Summary of Events and Information	Remarks and references to Appendices
CAESTRE	25/5/16		C. Section with additions from B. have been detailed to run this D.R.S. Lesson in order to get their hand in before the remainder are instructed. In case of a German attack, by orders from the A.D.M.S., I am to send two sections of 2 officers & 50 men, in each, in to Nos 138 T.A. and 115 others to Nos 140 1/2 T.A. Also 3 m. Ambulances to Nos 138 & 4 to Nos 140. Lieut. G. Bateman returns to-day from pass. 15 1/2 R & R.F.A.	Aped
"	26/5/16		A special message from General Joffre on the occasion of Empire Day expressing his sentiments of high esteem & cordial comradeship which the French Army feels for the Valiant troops of the Dominions & Colonies. Also a SPECIAL ORDER OF THE DAY. Congratulating the Royal Artillery on this the 300th year of their loyal government organization, for efficiency and support to other arms in every action in which they have been engaged.—	Aped
"	27/5/16		A cricket match V. The Canadian Divisional Train took place on our ground to-day in which we were beaten.	Aped
"	28/5/16		Parade Service 11 A.M. Evening Service 6-30 p.m. & 8-30 p.m.	Aped

No IX.

Army Form C. 2118

WAR DIARY
or
INTELLIGENCE SUMMARY
(Erase heading not required.)

MAY 1916

Place	Date	Hour	Summary of Events and Information	Remarks and references to Appendices
CAESTRE	29/5/16		Advance Party with Lieut. G. Bateman + A.J. Chiddingworth proceeded to BAILLEUL this morning. By orders from A.D.M.S. all returns from CAESTRE will be sent to me at BAILLEUL and a consolidated return forwarded from there to you A.D.M.S. Have placed Lieut. R.E. Jonker (S.R.) in charge of D.R.S. CAESTRE assisted by Lieut. T.T. Coveill (S.R.) Lieut. D.R. Yleman.	Seed.
BAILLEUL	30/5/16		The remainder of the Field Ambulance (A + B Sections) have taken over from the 2/1st Field Ambulance in D.R.S. BAILLEUL. In addition to the 4 tents operating and 8 tents C.S.I. I have put up 8 tents operating + 16 tents C.S.I. (this includes 12 tents of the 140% A.J.) orders given for 3 baths to be supplied daily to the Sanitary Officer arrangements have been made for a funeral "bearer party" to be provided when required by the O.C. S.P. in BAILLEUL, consisting of 1 Sergeant R.A.M.C. + 4 other R.A.M.C. and 12 convalescents.	Seed.
"	31/5/16		All my N.C.O's and men are billeted in the D.R.S. Saw the Transport Lieut. Major. Have obtained 10 cwt. of wood from the C.R.E. 41 Division for the purpose of making tables & other necessary articles, returned a fat. Sea long day Lieut. W.T. Wilson R.A.M.C. has returned for duty.	O.C. 125

1875 Wt. W593/826 1,000,000 4/15 J.B.C.&A. A.D.S.S./Forms/C.2118.

139. Amb.
Vol 2 June

139 F.A

Jan 14 16
S

From
  O.C. 139
  Field Ambulance
To
  Adjutant General
  Base
  B.E.F. France

Sir,
  I have the honour to submit herewith my War Diary for the month of June 1916.

  I have the honour to be
  Sir your obedient servant
  A.W. Long
  3/7/16. Major RAMC
  O.C. 139th Field Ambulance

VOLUME III

Army Form C. 2118

JUNE WAR DIARY 1916.
or
INTELLIGENCE SUMMARY
(Erase heading not required.)

Instructions regarding War Diaries and Intelligence Summaries are contained in F.S. Regs., Part II. and the Staff Manual respectively. Title Pages will be prepared in manuscript.

Place	Date	Hour	Summary of Events and Information	Remarks and references to Appendices
D.R.S. Advanced HQ BAILLEUL	1/6/16		Method of Evacuation when not in action by A.D.M.S. 41 Division. Motor cyclist orderly reaches H.Q., No 14 M.A.C. & No 11 a.m. daily for the Divisional stations & Nº 140 F.A. at Pont de Nieppe and Nº 138 F.A. at Steenwerck to ascertain how many patients (sitting & lying) require evacuation. At 2 p.m. daily motor ambulances will be sent to either station, if necessary to O.C. F.A. will wire to O.C. 14 M.A.C. an order stating number lying & sitting - and repeat message to A.D.M.S. II Corps. On M.A. Car of 14 M.A.C. conveys to BAILLEUL & relieves O.C. 14 M.A.C. will report cases to BAILLEUL & relieves arranged by the O.C. 14 M.A.C. INFECTIOUS CASES will be to 1st Canadian C.C.S. for ears. EYE CASES all to be sent due & from on to No 15 C.C.S. classified accordingly to rules laid down by the A.D.M.S.	Appx
"	2/6/16		The A.D.M.S. visited the D.R.S. Estaires, and also 1st D.R.S. at CAESTRE. Old NCO & men discharged from and new O.R.S. + 1st D.R.S. at CAESTRE on to report to the A.P.M's office in STEENWERCK.	Appx
"	3/6/16			Appx
"	4/6/16		By order Dixon O.C. 41 Division.	Appx

WAR DIARY or INTELLIGENCE SUMMARY

Army Form C. 2118

Place	Date	Hour	Summary of Events and Information	Remarks and references to Appendices
BAILLEUL	4 6/16		Major General S.T.P. Saunders C.B. Commanding 41st Division visited this Casualty Clearing Station to-day and was pleased with all arrangements. He was accompanied by the A.D.M.S. During the month of MAY we had only a few wet days.	
"	5 6/16		Bath arrangements are now being made for the bathing of patients as they come in, the washing & disinfection of their clothes, and the issue of a complete change of under-clothing. All the patients in this C.R.S. are now in tents, as is the wish of the D.D.M.S. II Corps. Those at D.R.S. CAESTRE are also in tents save a few severe cases as there are no further wards supplied to that station yet.	
"	6 6/16		This evening the patients and men were treated to a conjuring entertainment by Mr. A. Jessey Y.M.C.A. with gramophone selections.	
"	7 6/16		The King has issued with profound regret of the disaster by which the Secretary of State for War has lost his life while proceeding on a Special Mission to Russia.	

WAR DIARY or INTELLIGENCE SUMMARY

Army Form C. 2118

Place	Date	Hour	Summary of Events and Information	Remarks and references to Appendices
BAILLEUL	8/6/16		Lieut. R.J. Jobs has been detailed to take over the sanitary and medical supervision of the Young Officers training school whilst they are on this A.D.S. Has been divided up amongst the officers as follows: Lieut. Sheldon T.W. Adjutant, to supervise all medical & surgical stores. Lieut A.J. Chillingworth to supervise Reception Room, Dressing Station, Raft house and Linen Room. Lieut. S. Wilson to supervise the whole of the chateau with the exception of the dining hall & basement also S.A. equipment. Lieut G. Batman to supervise Cook house, Q.M. Stores, Motor Transport Room, Carpenters & tin smiths shop & wash house. Sergt R.J. Todd Sanitary Officer of D.R.S. Transport lines, and Young Officers training school.	Yes
"	9/6/16		Obtained sanction from Comdr. d'Etapes to have the drains connected up at the cook shop in the transport lines, and the cess-foot drained + filled in.	Yes

WAR DIARY
or
INTELLIGENCE SUMMARY
(Erase heading not required.)

Army Form C. 2118

Place	Date	Hour	Summary of Events and Information	Remarks and references to Appendices
BAILLEUL	10/6/16		2 wounded A.+D. Bookmakers on Yest various Colonial troops and British troops in France and Belgium. Yesterday is made out of all cases likely to be for some time **Temporarily Unfit** & **Permanently Unfit** & all men passing from R.R.S. the A.D.M.S. inspects those on Saturdays and orders them either T.U. or P.B. Those marked T.U. are sent to the Camp Commandant at Steenwerck, P.B. those marked P.B. are sent to the Base to be dealt with there. Parade Service 9-30 a.m.	ans.
"	11/6/16			
"	12/6/16		Medical Conference at Steenwerck. Rest by yet ADMS. 41 Divn. Remain steadily all day. An NCO & 10 men sent to 140 F.A. for instructional purposes for the day. An NCO + 7 men to report daily to the C.A.D.O.S. for work. A fatigue party of 20 men sent to the Town Incinerators to load our wagons with ashes and time for the purpose of filling up a large cess-pit in our tent-field.	gtd.
"	13/6/16		The Rev. J. Thomas C.F. Res Cupt 15 joins H.Q. 123rd Inf. Bde.	ans.

WAR DIARY
or
INTELLIGENCE SUMMARY
(Erase heading not required.)

Army Form C. 2118

Place	Date	Hour	Summary of Events and Information	Remarks and references to Appendices
BAILLEUL	13/6/15		Our guide, one of Typhoid inoculated to 1 Canadian C.C.S. a P.U. of 605 conj. M.M. A.S.C. who was in a tent at point 27.W.6.C.2.1. of this coy. has since moved to some unknown place, being disposed of the farm.	Aut
"	14/6/15		PROTECTION OF AID-POSTS. All dug-outs & cellars on cleared rooms occupied as regimental aid-posts or A.D.S's will be gratefully properly constructed. Sans with blankets hung in such a way as to be easily adapted to open at once when lit for alarm sounds & the blankets should be daily sprayed with solution & instantly when a gas attack is imminent, by order from A.D.M.S.	Aut
"	15/6/15		VERMORAL SPRAYERS. On gas alarm, R.A.P. cellar or A.D.S with two refills of solution Sodium hyposulphite — to 1½ oz ¾ oz on this Carbonate — 4 oz 3 on 1½ muslin. Water — gals 3	Aut
"	16/6/15			Aut
"	17/6/15		Private VERBAUWEDE has been granted leave till 26th inst. A wiring preparations & ... + no tellico available made on this form "15" T 15" indicating antitetanic serum, 1500 or 1500 units, also A for antitoxin + M for antitoxin ...	Aut

WAR DIARY
or
INTELLIGENCE SUMMARY
(Erase heading not required.)

Army Form C. 2118

Place	Date	Hour	Summary of Events and Information	Remarks and references to Appendices
BAILLEUL	18/6/16		The A.D.M.S. & D.A.D.M.S. visited A.R.S. CAESTRE today. Parade service in the Chateau at 11-30 a.m.	Hist.
"	19/6/16		Major General St. B. Lanford C.B. commanding 41 Division visited the D.R.S. today.	Hist
"	20/6/16		A similar a daily return will be sent to the A.D.M.S. as follows ADMITTED SICK ADMITTED WOUNDED EVACUATED SICK EVACUATED WOUNDED LYING DOWN SITTING CESS PIT filled in & drain pipes connected up.	Hist
"	21/6/16		Visited A.R.S. CAESTRE today and found everything progressing satisfactorily.	Hist
"	22/6/16		Visited the A.D.S. 140¹²/⁴ A. and A.D.S.'s of the 138²/⁴ & 140¹²/⁴ A. & inspected several of the roads as to their condition for motor Ambulances & cycles.	Hist
"	23/6/16		Have had Cook House generally cleant washed & whitened. Spent the day arranging kits for yr. mun's gases & equipment.	Hist
"	24/6/16		Visited A.R.S. CAESTRE and arranged for 2 NCO's & 2B to proceed to A.R.S. BAILLEUL on 25th in order to be ready on duties as required by the A.D.M.S. 41. division.	Hist
"	25/6/16		Parade service at 9-30 a.m.	Hist

WAR DIARY or INTELLIGENCE SUMMARY

Army Form C. 2118

Place	Date	Hour	Summary of Events and Information	Remarks and references to Appendices
	26/6/16		Instead of distributing the sick among the Field Ambulances as at present, all cases on Bidets are sent direct to 4 A. receiving casualties who deal with them as follows (1) Return them to Duty (2) send them to No 12 C.C.S. (3) Put cases to D/O 2 C.C.S. except on Wednesday & Saturday when they are sent to D/O 1 C.C.S. EXCEPT T Ingestion cases which are dealt with as follows:- the Regimental M.O. notifies the case to O.C. 4 F.A., the O.C. 4 F.A. notifies the Rd. Isolation Hospital (I.C.C.S.) giving any reference of case, and the R.S.M. sends an ambulance for the case which the O.C. his unit arranges with the O.C. No 8 C.C.S.	West
	27/6/16		50 men & 2 N.C.O's have proceeded to Am. to report to Officer i/c A.D.S. 138th Field Ambulance for fatigue duty. Taking with them 10 days rations and the unexpired portion of today's rations, and also their own Rations.	West
	28/6/16		Lieut R.I. Graham R.A.M.C. has taken over his duties as 2nd in Command at A.R.S. BAILLEUL from Lieut T.W. Shelton who has proceeded to CAESTRE for duty. Lieut R.I. Graham handed over the A.R.S. CAESTRE to Lieut F. Corkill.	West

WAR DIARY
or
INTELLIGENCE SUMMARY
(Erase heading not required.)

Army Form C. 2118

Instructions regarding War Diaries and Intelligence Summaries are contained in F.S. Regs., Part II. and the Staff Manual respectively. Title Pages will be prepared in manuscript.

Place	Date	Hour	Summary of Events and Information	Remarks and references to Appendices
BAILLEUL	28/6		Lieut. G. Boltman R.A. has detailed to report himself to O.C. 132nd Brigade R.F.A. at NNWPE 13.b.C.18 for duty. Began in relief of Lieut. Reardon J.T. R.A.M.C. who will report to O.C. 135 F.A. Jn Auth/ of the 20th	
	29/6		Lieut. R.S. Garvey & Wilson and myself visited the new A.D.S. which is being made by our men on the PLOEGSTEERT - HYDE PARK CORNER Rd. Reconnoitred Hill 63 + viewed the surrounding from the top.	
	30/6		a beautiful clear day. 14 hostile aeroplanes manoeuvering over head. Orders have been given from the A.D.S. en S. to cut down our no of patients on this A.D.S. to 100 and start at CAESTRE. on this A.D.S. to 100 and start at CAESTRE included. 20 to have to Rue + 20 at CAESTRE.	
			INGO + 15 men have been sent, 1 Major from G.S. en S. + 1 Lieut from Corps to m.O.S. to take the place of O.C. 140 St.A. Arch there will arrive tomorrow to take charge of our patients under O.C. 138 F.A.	
			His Lordsp Major R.A.M.C. O.C. 139 M2 Field Ambulance	

4L July
vol 3

CONFIDENTIAL

St John Amb
139th Beer Ambulance

COMMITTEE FOR THE
MEDICAL HISTORY OF THE WAR
Date 5 - SEP 1915

Volume III
July 1916

VOLUME No III   JULY 1916.   WAR DIARY or INTELLIGENCE SUMMARY   Army Form C. 2118

Place	Date	Hour	Summary of Events and Information	Remarks and references to Appendices
BAILLEUL	1/7/16		Lieut T.D. Elder has proceeded to take over charge of our fatigue party under O.C. 12th F.A. and one N.C.O. & 15 men have been sent to report to O.C. 140th F.A. by orders from the A.D.M.S.	Yesterday
"	2/7/16		Lieut C. Cameron R.A.M.C. has reported this day for duty. Form G.1054.	Yesterday
"	3/7/16		Parade service 9-30 a.m. Visited Hill 63 with Lieut Joseph & Wilson.	Yesterday
"	4/7/16		Lieut R.J. Joseph & Lt Corbett have been promoted Captain - dated July 1st 1916.	Yesterday
"	5/7/16		Visited the reserve trenches & a Ry. and Post with Lieut Cameron in order to instruct him in the present war-fare. We also visited an A.D.S. and one under construction All cattle Ambulances are now to be protected with a border layer of chicken wire.	Yesterday
"	6/7/16		Lieut A.J. Chillingworth has exchanged with Lieut S.F. Thomas at Caestre.	Yesterday
"	7/7/16		All tents are being painted various colours, as protection against air craft.	Yesterday
"	8/7/16		Sergt. A Hayton R.A.M.C. has proceeded, by order, to report to the A.D.M.S. 9th A. today.	Yesterday

WAR DIARY
or
INTELLIGENCE SUMMARY

Army Form C. 2118

(Erase heading not required.)

Place	Date	Hour	Summary of Events and Information	Remarks and references to Appendices
BAILLEUL	10/7/16	10.7 / 11.16	Lieut. Wilson Orr proceeded to CAESTRE for Bully. In the morning at 5 minutes to three fire broke out in the Stables. Immediately fire was broken out in the Marines camp and immediately role was alarm but in spite of all that the stables were completely burnt. Most of the Horses some of the 21 horses who were missing after the fire have been found in the fields and farms about.	Ibid. Ibid.
"	12/7/16		A court of Enquiry on the burning of the Stables was held. The cause of which could not be established and as far as we could find it is attached to anyone. The President was Major T. Mc. J. Jarvis 10 R.W.S.	Ibid.
"	13/7/16			Ibid.
"	14/7/16		Under orders received from the Q.Q.M.S. 42446 C/M Hallon reported to Q.Q.M.S. Q.H.Q. 12 Echelon on July 9/12 (Orders continued)	Ibid.
"	15/7/16		Special orders were issued today to the Officers & men by order and others general as regards, sick & wounded officers. Church Parade 9-30 A.M. All my horses have now been found.	Ibid.
"	16/7/16		All lights are to be extinguished, or properly screened in all rooms by 9 p.m. until further orders.	Ibid.

WAR DIARY
or
INTELLIGENCE SUMMARY
(Erase heading not required.)

Army Form C. 2118

Place	Date	Hour	Summary of Events and Information	Remarks and references to Appendices
BAILLEUL	17/7/16		Promotions. Acting appointments without pay. 14653 t/Cpl Owen A/S. to be A/Sgr. 705 41 Pte Butterfield to be t/Cpl. 66 941 Cpl Pilton V. to be t/Sgt. 14829 Pte Bailey to be t/Cpl. 66177 A/Cpl Bentley S.S. to be A/Sgt. Pte A/Cpl Thompson Glen 4/12/16.	Hut
"	18/7/16		Latest A.R.O. 1653 Military Service — Civil liabilities need not be attended to.	Hut
"	19/7/16		All ordnance stores which the ordnance have been unable to supply can be obtained from the H.Q. R.A.M.C. Corps Coy. on application from the A.D.M.S. All other necessaries to enable a D.R.S. 2 comportable for the men can be obtained from the Red Cross Society or in situ.	Hut
"	20/7/16		All our available men have been working all day to till 12 mid night carrying wounded from ambulances to train the following attentions in the D.R.S. have been made today. C.O. office & a large room on 1st landing with clerks office over door, Q.M. stores to be in room right of entrance. Receiving Room to be in room on right of entrance. Medical Inspection to be in [illegible] —	Hut

WAR DIARY or INTELLIGENCE SUMMARY

Army Form C. 2118

Place	Date	Hour	Summary of Events and Information	Remarks and references to Appendices
BAILLEUL	21/7/16		Have sent some 15 officers into billeted to give assistance, and also a reliable instruction for N.C.O's. Lieut. ?? Wilkinson is now acting as Q.M.?. The large cragh in the convent of our Tent Field has now undergone into a vegetable & flower garden.	Hart
"	22/7/16		Field ambulances inspected by A.D.M.S. today. At present we established of a Field Ambulance is 6 officers 10 A.S.C. (H.T.) 36 R.A.M.C of ??? ??? 159 A.S.C. (M.T.) 14 R.A.M.C. of ??? ??? 192	
			*Includes 1 A.S.C. Train Transport. Surplus A.S.C. (H.T.) 1, A.S.C. (M.T.) 3, R.A.M.C. (T.F.) + 47½ Total 51	Hart
"	28/7/16		Church parade 9-30 a.m. By order from the A.D.M.S. any wounded rear station are not to exceed 200 all together. No case is to be kept here more than 10 days. All cases requiring more than 10 days treatment will be sent on to ?? except cases requiring more than 2 weeks treatment ↗ ↙ which are sent to the C.C.S.	Hart

WAR DIARY
or
INTELLIGENCE SUMMARY
(Erase heading not required.)

Army Form C. 2118

Place	Date	Hour	Summary of Events and Information	Remarks and references to Appendices
BAILLEUL	23/7/16		continued. Every man transferred to A.D.R.S. evacuated to C.C.S. on discharged to duty must be certified daily to oc unit concerned	that
"	24/7/16		A.R.S. visited to-day by the D.D.M.S. Lt Col Ho/Himro Col McCallaghan who expressed his satisfaction with everything concerned and suggested clearing of the patients, & Rahnse rooms & Cook house for fight 4th S.C.	that
"	25/7/16		Visited by Col. J.S. Knox A.A. + Q.M.G. re the Rivoir beds of a R.A.M.C. exam.	that
"			Under him the A.D.M.S. Lieut. R.T. & 88 R.A.M.C. has ordered to-day to take over from Lieut C. Scott the duties of M.O. to VT 202 Wullman L.G. and Lieut C. Scott has received his orders.	that
"	26/7/16		Visited the A.R.S. CAESTRE on the 232d again to-day	that
"	27/7/16		Both am. D.R. S. were visited again by VT. J.M.S. D. Army who expressed his satisfaction with everything. He was accompanied by the A.D.M.S. 41st Division, and recommended accommodation for 100 patients at CAESTRE and 100 at BAILLEUL.	that

Army Form C. 2118

WAR DIARY
or
INTELLIGENCE SUMMARY
(Erase heading not required.)

Instructions regarding War Diaries and Intelligence Summaries are contained in F. S. Regs., Part II. and the Staff Manual respectively. Title Pages will be prepared in manuscript.

Place	Date	Hour	Summary of Events and Information	Remarks and references to Appendices
BAILLEUL	28/7/16		It has been found that in order to keep our patients down to 200 it is necessary to evacuate down to 100 before end of M day.	Apd
"	29/7/16		The A.R.S. CAESTRE was visited by one J.D.M.S. Letter & he expressed his satisfaction to the Officer i/c A Colonel (name not yet known) also inspected the D.R.S. and recommended an increase to be built the same as the one in the A.R.S. Railroad — with a cover to the one A.D.M.S. has granted doubts for in skeleton	Apd
"	30/7/16		Sunday. Church Parade 9.30 A.M. Usual weekly Conference. A discussion on the medical arrangements doubts. Steel helmets should never fear out of a divisional area.	Apd
"	31/7/16		This morning hear him very fine, with only a few user days. The 138th F.A. is still at STEENWERCK and the 140th F.A. at PONT de NIEPPE.	Apd

WAR DIARY
or
INTELLIGENCE SUMMARY

Army Form C. 2118

Place	Date	Hour	Summary of Events and Information	Remarks and references to Appendices
BAILLEUL	31/1/16		The following is the present arrangement for the disposal of **SICK & WOUNDED OFFICERS** in the Division	Yes
			All cases in GHQ giving line, or such as are sent direct to Field Ambulances receiving Casualties are dealt with them as follows:—	
			1. Return them to duty.	
			2. If likely to be fit in 10 days are sent to No 2 C.C.S. BAILLEUL.	
			3. Send them to No 2 C.C.S. BAILLEUL.	
			4. Eye Cases, to No 15 C.C.S. HAZEBROUCK.	
			✱ EXCEPT on WEDNESDAYS & SATURDAYS, when Cases for No 2 C.C.S. are sent to the 1st Canadian C.C.S. in BAILLEUL.	
			EXCEPT. I. "INFECTIOUS CASES" which are dealt with as follows— The Regimental m.o. notifies the case to O.C. Field Ambulance the O.C. F.A. notifies the BRITISH ISOLATION HOSPITAL (1st Canadian C.C.S.) giving M.O. infrce of case, and the B.T.H. sends an ambulance for the case.	
			II. "DENTAL CASES". The m.o. of his unit arranges an appointment with the O.C. NORTH MIDLAND CASUALTY C.S. MONT DES CATS.	

WAR DIARY or INTELLIGENCE SUMMARY

Army Form C. 2118

Place	Date	Hour	Summary of Events and Information	Remarks and references to Appendices
BAILLEUL			Disposal of Sick & Wounded of C.O.s & men belonging to 4th & 2nd Division. All cases on sick lines or billets are sent direct to St Jude Ambulance receiving casualties who deal with them as follows:— 1. Return them to duty. 2. Slightly sick or injured are put into billets within 48 hours are admitted 3. sent to A.R.S. BAILLEUL. who sick are sent within 14 days are sent to A.R.S. BAILLEUL. 4. SEVERE CASES. who are or likely to be ill within 14 days, are sent to C.C.S. BAILLEUL receiving for one day. 5. DENTAL CASES, sent to A.R.S.; from there going to Harbonnières ex-HAZEBROUCK to NORTH MIDLAND C.C.S. MONT des CATS., each morning 6. EYE CASES, sent to A.R.S. from there going to No 15.C.C.S HAZEBROUCK every Tuesday morning & to A.D.m.S. being advised by A.R.S. by 4 pm on Wednesday the total number of cases requiring evacuation. 7. SCABIES CASES, sent to A.R.S. by file 12 noon daily & A.R.S. advise at 7.am O BAILLEUL the number of cases requiring evacuation.	Yet

1875 Wt. W593/826 1,000,000 4/15 J.B.C. & A. A.D.S.S./Forms/C. 2118.

WAR DIARY
or
INTELLIGENCE SUMMARY
(Erase heading not required.)

Army Form C. 2118

Place	Date	Hour	Summary of Events and Information	Remarks and references to Appendices
BAILLEUL	7 continued		the A.M.O. gives the time of Guns and the cases are then sent by rail to No 50 C.C.S. HAZEBROUCK for temporary treatment, we being advised when the men are discharged to duty, or evacuated to the Base.	Yes.
			8. Permanent Base or Venereal Until men are sent to A.R.S. on Friday and are kept Arf lalle the A.D.M.S. every Saturday morning. These men recommended as P.B. are sent to Ry Sta BAILLEUL, travelling by rail to their various Base Depots; J.W. men being sent to Camp Commandant, STEENWERCK for further duty.	
			9. Infectious Cases the eye. M.O. notifies the case to the O.C. nearest H.A. giving every reference of case. He O.C. H.A. notifies the British Gobbe Hospl, furnishing reference of case and also O.C. the A.T. and Ambulance sent care the O.C. H.A. and repeats the wire to A.D.M.S. 41 Div. H.D. Cm S. V. Corps.	

Yrs Very Major R.A.M.C.
O.C. 139½ Field Ambulance

41st Div
Vol 4

COMMITTEE FOR THE
MEDICAL HISTORY OF THE WAR
Date −5 OCT. 1915

August 1916.
Confidential
War Diary
of
134th Field Amb
Aug 1st 1916 to Aug 31st 1916
Volume 4

WAR DIARY or INTELLIGENCE SUMMARY

Army Form C. 2118

VOL. V. AUGUST 1916.

ORDERLY ROOM
1 SEP. 1916
No. A.394/16
139th FIELD AMBULANCE

Place	Date	Hour	Summary of Events and Information	Remarks and references to Appendices
BAILLEUL	1/8/16		Lieut. E. Cameron R.A.M.C. has taken over the duties of Lieut. C. Scott in addition to his own, pending holiday, when Lieut. C. Scott reported himself for duty to O.C. D.R.S. CAESTRE.	Her.
"	2/8/16		The D.D.M.S. V Corps has decided that the Corps House is too over the latrines in the 3 R.S. CAESTRE. Plans arranged to remove the cookhouse to a more distant spot.	Her.
"	3/8/16		Visited today the old & new A.D.S of the 140th H.A. & the new A.D.S of the 135th H.A.	Her.
"	4/8/16		Rd. Dental Crew Officers + men Reg A.B. on our right. The A.D.S of the 135th H.A. All crew went to No.2.C.C.S. (AUSTRALIAN) TROIS ARBRES.	her.
"	5/8/16		Visited CAESTRE D.R.S. with a view to ensuring better arrangements of the winter.	her
"	6/8/16		Lieut W.T. Wilson has taken over charge of the 2nd pr party from Lieut J.W. Sheldon who has returned to D.R.S. CAESTRE. for duty. Capt. J.H. C. Webb has relieved Lieut. W.T. Wilson	her
"	7/8/16		at the A.D.S of 135th H.A. Lieut. D.P. Thomas has taken over from CAPT. R.E. Smiley at A.D.S. 14.02 H.A. + CAPT R.E. Smiley has returned to duty to D.R.S. Baillul	

WAR DIARY
or
INTELLIGENCE SUMMARY
(Erase heading not required.)

Army Form C. 2118

Place	Date	Hour	Summary of Events and Information	Remarks and references to Appendices
BAILLEUL	8/9/16		Field Ambulance will supply an O. C. the Units with Mule-Compts. A.D.S. the Rear Game. They will keep a charge on all subsequent issues and report on any excess medical & surgical material will also be issued as required according to orders from A.D.M.S. I have detailed Lieut. C. Cameron to take over medical charge of No Bombing Schools of the 122nd, 123rd + 12 + 2 Inft. Bde. from to-day. Plans submitted this day, showing the A.A. S.M.S. Hospital, the A.D.M.S. a advanced dressing station, and the proposed arrangements for WINTER QUARTERS of my A.D.S., BAILLEUL & at CAESTRE, including the winter arrangements	Yes
"	9/9/16			nil
"	10/9/16		Have erected a Water Tank with cover in the Tent field. Visited the Bombing School of the 122 & 123 grs. 13 ex.- the A.D.S. + Shelters at PLOEGSTEERT WOOD and the front line of trenches with Lieut. C. Cameron.	Yes

WAR DIARY or INTELLIGENCE SUMMARY

Army Form C. 2118

Place	Date	Hour	Summary of Events and Information	Remarks and references to Appendices
BAILLEUL	11/6/16.		The O.C. 138th F.A. has handed over the A.D.S. ROMARIN. (map 36. B.4.a.6) on 27/7/16. to a F.A. of the 36th Div. The following shews the number of killed, wounded, missing and wounded sick during the months of June & July, 1916. in the 4th Division, including all medical units.	Hug

OFFICERS   OTHER RANKS

		KILLED	WOUNDED	MISSING	KILLED	WOUNDED	MISSING	EVACUATED SICK
June		5	21	1	99	432	–	257
July		6	43	–	120	665	19	262
				of these shew field ambulances only.				
June {	138	–	–	–	–	–	–	1
	139	–	–	–	1	–	–	4
	140	–	–	–	–	–	–	1
July {	138	–	–	–	–	–	–	1
	139	–	–	–	–	–	–	5
	140	–	–	–	–	–	–	5

Hug

WAR DIARY
or
INTELLIGENCE SUMMARY
(Erase heading not required.)

Army Form C. 2118

Place	Date	Hour	Summary of Events and Information	Remarks and references to Appendices
BAILLEUL	10/5/16		Procedure when sick & wounded N.C.Os & men belonging to or attached to H15 & Divis. are admitted to 9th H15 Divisional Rest Stations. The sick & receiving orderlies examines patients & if not D.R.S.W. likely to be fit for duty in a period not exceeding 10 days is sent back to the vicinity of the D.R.S. also sent with grummy sick and on arrival has been by the orderly officer of the day. All cases admitted & sent to the receiving room ditto 44°, are shown a D.A. cases, and transferred to the D.R.S. or the close of the day. On being transferred to the D.R.S. the patients report at the admission & inspection Room where they are examined by the orderly on O, and is admitted to the D.R.S. for treatment, duty re fit each is noted on the admission slip (A for A. 315 (A was medical card) a copy given) A+D. Room obtains full particulars from patients as they arrive which are entered daily	Not Not

Place	Date	Hour	Summary of Events and Information	Remarks and references to Appendices
BAILLEUL		III	On the A.M. Report (A.F. 27 A.) should a case be a severe one, it is mentioned that O.C. S. receiving for the days states, that N.C.O. i/c giving them a receipt for same on A.F. 1F2 (Hospital Pass Store Ledger for R) the N.C.O. ascertains that they seem have each a towel, soap, + hold all complete for their convenience. Should the patients have any valuables they wish taken care of, they are handed to the Pack Store N.C.O. and a receipt given on A.F. 191 (Hospital Receipt Book, Patient's valuables) and the articles of clothing handed in to the Q.M. Stores.	Nil
"		IV	When the kit bags are handed onto store, and receipt obtained the patient reports to the N.C.O. i/c Batt Home Standing over their A.F.W. 3118, to get N.C.O. i/c signing his name certifying that the men have duly had a bath, + have also been supplied with clean between clothing. During the time that patients are bathing, the seams of their coats + trousers &c are gone over with hot flame irons, thus reducing the possibility of bringing live into the D.V. S. to a minimum, + doctors also descend	Nil

WAR DIARY
or
INTELLIGENCE SUMMARY
(Erase heading not required.)

Army Form C. 2118

Place	Date	Hour	Summary of Events and Information	Remarks and references to Appendices
BAILLEUL		V	only patients then report to the Battn. Shops + transport to have a share, low cost or over attendance is, as may be necessary, with patients when so to their tents or marquees allotted to them, and their lying on straw A.L.S. 3118, to which is given blanket and are handed over regularly on the surgical on medical side.	Nil
"		VI	The duty slave M.O. to M.C. to within A.R. or "A" is a general duty, the patients talking the meals in the Dining Mess "R" to "A" Glar ordered	Nil
		VII	C.O. will visit the patients resident to their beds	
"		VIII	Each orderly keeps a nominal roll of all patients under his charge in his care book which shows each man by No. Rank, Name, Regt., Diagnosis & treatment of case and disposal.	Nil
"		IX	with orderly parade for men for the C.O.'s orders or I'm daily the M.O. O'clays is necessary the treatment or diet changed the M.O. so combines dictates which is noted should be evacuated to the C.C.S. The orderly orderlies a note against the names on his case book as in the disposal column. Later inform the M.O. 80 (N.D. or C.C.S.)	Nil

1875 Wt. W593/826 1,000,000 4/15 J.B.C. & A. A.D.S.S./Forms/C. 2118.

WAR DIARY
or
INTELLIGENCE SUMMARY

Army Form C. 2118

Place	Date	Hour	Summary of Events and Information	Remarks and references to Appendices
BAILLEUL	X		If after a period of 10 days not to R.d. treatment is not fit for duty, but if likely to be fit in another 7/10 days, he cannot use long c.c.s. sheet-dur-cat-you admit accordingly the same procedure as above.	April
"	XI		divided the M.O. consider a patient to be unfit for permanent duties, the man is recommended as being S/little G.S. (Commandant Room) or T.u. (temporary unfit)	May
"	XII		The total orderlies other than those employed at the offices Last clerk, mess, operating theatre mess, quarter-man-cats etc, compiled on A.4.W. completing the A & D. Room, sent to be evacuated etc. — the A & D. Book divide on receipt of A.M.W. 3200 between nominal rolls for the men going to c.c.s or ments-dur-cat.	
"	XIII		The patients may be admitted to the c.c.s. receiving for the day at any time.	May

Place	Date	Hour	Summary of Events and Information	Remarks and references to Appendices
BAILLEUL			Three for M.C.C.S. must be left, must arrive there before 12 noon. The wounded men to continue dressing the patients at 11-15 a.m. The patients are shown by the M.O. a M.O. for duty are not discharged until the following day. Six the men from the 4 & 3 from Clerk advises the O.C. unit of the men being discharged the the following day the men for duty are paraded at 1 p.m. and the Area Ambulance takes them to the A.P.M's office at NIEPPE where guides for the various units are sent to conduct the men to quarters occupied by their units. Men for duty of the other division are sent to the R.T.O. Bailleul Station. A nominal Roll is rendered to the R.N.O. on the previous evening, who notifies us no what time train the men are to travel by.	Apph
"		XV	Dental cases are sent to No 2. Australian C.C.S. between the hours of 9 + 12 and 2 + 4 daily. A nominal nell in duplicate is sent with the Ambulance car orderly, the duplicate of each man being shown on the duplicate nell which is returned continued	Apph

Army Form C. 2118

WAR DIARY
or
INTELLIGENCE SUMMARY
(Erase heading not required.)

Place	Date	Hour	Summary of Events and Information	Remarks and references to Appendices
BAILLEUL		XVI	On the afternoon of a case of scabies but S.R.S. the patient takes all his kit with him and the ward amalgam our own in the tent set aside for scabies case. They are sent by rail daily to No 50 C.C.S. for temporary treatment. We notify the I.M.O. Railway Station daily stating the number of cases for evacuation, who notifies in the train which the case are to travel. On a man being discharged to duty in evacuated to base No 50 C.C.S. inform the A.D.M.S. who in turn notifies us.	(Aps)
		XVIII	The total number of Bys taken for evacuation from the D.R.S. to No 15 X C.C.S. are noted. the A.D.m.S. by 4 for real warning. The motor ambulance convoy collecting the cases by the following morning at 7 a.m. & taking them to No 15 - C.C.S. a nominal roll in duplicate accompanies all cases, its disposal of each case being shown on this duplicate roll, which is returned to us. continued.	(Aps)

WAR DIARY
or
INTELLIGENCE SUMMARY
(Erase heading not required.)

Army Form C. 2118

Instructions regarding War Diaries and Intelligence Summaries are contained in F.S. Regs., Part II. and the Staff Manual respectively. Title Pages will be prepared in manuscript.

Place	Date	Hour	Summary of Events and Information	Remarks and references to Appendices
BAILLEUL		XVIII	The D.A.D.M.S. makes a nominal Roll of all men proposed for Permanent Base & temporary unfit men to the A. + D. Room and 6 p.m. Friday, the A. + D. Room notifying the office, where a nominal roll in duplicate is prepared for the A.D.M.S. at following morning at 10 a.m. The men then get the medical board on Saturday but send results of 9-50 a.m. on each Saturday. There are still recommended for the Base are sent to the Rfd. This Rendezvous for distants to their various Base Depôts. The Cases totally obtained from the D.M.O. & those who are going to U.K. on sent to the Comp't-Commandant STEENWERCK, for disposal, a nominal roll giving all particulars accompanying the men in both cases.	Not
"		XIX	Inspection seen on shown as admitted into the D.R.S. on the A. + D. book only, no case being actually admitted to the Unit.	Not

continued

WAR DIARY
or
INTELLIGENCE SUMMARY
(Erase heading not required.)

Army Form C. 2118

Place	Date	Hour	Summary of Events and Information	Remarks and references to Appendices
BAILLEUL		XX	Should a patient contract a disease which has not shown by his 2nd. or. card. The particulars are immediately reported to the A. & D. Room	Hus
"		XXI	Venereal Cases are always reported to the A.S.M. should the case have been contracted in France or Belgium the men to report here until the A.D.M. Can investigate the case. If the case has been contracted in England a report to that effect to given to the Vet. m. O. when escorting him the case to the A.D.M.	Hus Hickory cayor R.a.m.c.

WAR DIARY
or
INTELLIGENCE SUMMARY
(Erase heading not required.)

Army Form C. 2118

Instructions regarding War Diaries and Intelligence Summaries are contained in F.S. Regs., Part II and the Staff Manual respectively. Title Pages will be prepared in manuscript.

Place	Date	Hour	Summary of Events and Information	Remarks and references to Appendices
BAILLEUL	13/6/16	9-30 a.m.	Church Parade. Received orders to hand over D.R.S. CAESTRE on the 14/12 inst. and D.R.S. BAILLEU on the 18/12 also orders re. entrainment on the 23rd inst.	appx
"	14/6/16			appx
"	15/6/16		Received orders to hand over motor Ambulances to O.C. 70th F.A. relieving unit - except 3 to be retained till re entrain. Lieut. W. Wilson has returned with fatigue party of his party has done most excellent work in making R.A.P.'s & A.D.S. Lieut. R.J. Todd has returned, being relieved by Lieut. R.m. Scott.	appx
"	16/6/16			appx
"	17/6/16		Capt. T.A. Curzie has handed over the D.R.S. CAESTRE to O.C. 70th Field Ambulance. And has proceeded to billets in a farm at 29.X.1.6.3.3	appx
"	18/6/16		Have handed over D.R.S. BAILLEUL to O.C. 70th F.A. Amber and proceeded to 29.X.1.6.33. in VST movt. des cats area.	appx
29.X.1.6.33	19/6/16		Old limber wagon to be provided with crates for carrying petrol tins for water - These are the best form billets we have had.	appx

WAR DIARY or INTELLIGENCE SUMMARY

Army Form C. 2118

Place	Date	Hour	Summary of Events and Information	Remarks and references to Appendices
27 X It 33. BAILLEUL	6/9/16		The following is a list [summary] of the improvements which a D.R.S. can be worked, when all improvements have been made:	(list)
			Hospital for 200 men Tents NCO's + men R.A.M.C. 12	
			Clerks office & O.C. " 4	
			O.C. an. office + stores " 4	
			Cook house " 5	
			Sanitary squad " 6	
			Officers Servants " 2	
			Pack store " 3	
			Medical Inspection Room " 2	
			Dispensary " 2	
			Receiving Room " 3	
			Bath Squad " 2	
			Bath House + Clean Clothes Room " 6	
			Police 1 " 2	
			General duty 1 "	
			Visiting Inspector 1 " 1	
			Sergts. Mess 1 "	
			Incinerator "	

Army Form C. 2118

WAR DIARY
or
INTELLIGENCE SUMMARY
(Erase heading not required.)

Instructions regarding War Diaries and Intelligence Summaries are contained in F.S. Regs., Part II. and the Staff Manual respectively. Title Pages will be prepared in manuscript.

Place	Date	Hour	Summary of Events and Information	Remarks and references to Appendices
27X.1.6.33 BAILLEUL	19/16		continued Bargage Orderlies — NCOs & men R.A.M.C. 2.	Here
			Officers orderlies — " " " " " " " 1	
			Barbers — " " " " " " " 1	
			Rool makers — " " " " " " " "	
			Tailors — " " " " " " " "	
			Incinerator — " " " " " " " "	
			Carpenters — " " " " " " " "	
			Tin smith — " " " " " " " "	
			Dining Hall orderly — " " " " " " " "	
			Orderly Sergeant — " W.O. " 1	
			Sergt Major — " " " " " " 1	
			Orderly Post man — " " " " " " 4	
			Funeral Party — " " " " " " 5.	
			Additional help can be obtained from patients doing light duty	

Army Form C. 2118

WAR DIARY
or
INTELLIGENCE SUMMARY
(Erase heading not required.)

Instructions regarding War Diaries and Intelligence Summaries are contained in F.S. Regs., Part II. and the Staff Manual respectively. Title Pages will be prepared in manuscript.

Place	Date	Hour	Summary of Events and Information			Remarks and references to Appendices
			DAILY, WEEKLY, MONTHLY, & QUARTERLY RETURNS			
			SUBJECT		TO WHOM	
27/6.33 BAILLEUL	5/16	SUNDAY				
		MONDAY				
		TUESDAY	6 p.m. Certificat Re state of from Rations and Gas Helmets.		A.D.M.S.	
		WEDNESDAY	Offence Report A.F.B. 2069.		Q.D.M.S.	
			4 p.m. WIRE 2YE Cases for removal		A.D.M.S.	
		THURSDAY	9 A.m. Wives & Officers & Quarters on Leave Roll — Absentee Return 6 p.m.		D.H.Q A.D.M.S.	
		FRIDAY				
		SATURDAY	9 A.m. Nominal Roll of Officers first sanitation members of Committee 9 A.m. Return showing Motor ambulances required		A.D.M.S. A.D.M.S.	
			12 Noon W.D.A Return A.F.B. 23		A.D.M.S.	
			12 Noon Return of A&D. Strength A.D.M.S.		A.B.Coo	

Army Form C. 2118

WAR DIARY
or
INTELLIGENCE SUMMARY
(Erase heading not required.)

Instructions regarding War Diaries and Intelligence Summaries are contained in F.S. Regs., Part II. and the Staff Manual respectively. Title Pages will be prepared in manuscript.

Place	Date	Hour	Summary of Events and Information	Remarks and references to Appendices
21.1.1.33 a/6 BAILLEUL	6/6		Continued -	
			DAILY SUBJECT To whom	
		9 A.m.	Daily wire for evacuation not sent. A.D.M.S.	
		1.0 pm	State of sick + wounded & & W. 3185 wife to men for guarding at Bpo. A.D.M.S.	
			Notification of admission and evacuation of men of this division to be sent direct to 9th A.D.M.S. concerned by wire in practice. A.D.M.S. concerned	Hus
		6 pm	Casualty Return (evacuated) from units. Wire A.D.M.S.	

Army Form C. 2118

WAR DIARY
or
INTELLIGENCE SUMMARY
(Erase heading not required.)

Instructions regarding War Diaries and Intelligence Summaries are contained in F. S. Regs., Part II. and the Staff Manual respectively. Title Pages will be prepared in manuscript.

Place	Date	Hour	Summary of Events and Information	Remarks and references to Appendices
29X.1.b.33 BAILLEUL 19/6/16			continued:-	
			MONTHLY. SUBJECT. TO WHOM.	
	18/6	9 am	Return of R² Red X Stores drawn during preceding month.	A.D.M.S.
	20/6	6 pm	Return of Motor Cars & Cycles fit to take field.	A.D.M.S. AW
	27/6	6 pm	Return of horses in possession	A.D.M.S.
	29/6	9 am	Return of Motor Cars A.F.W. 3156	A.D.M.S.
	29/6	9 am	Return of Motor Cycles A.F.W. 3156. Claims for working pay (if any)	A.D.M.S.
	Last day	9 am	Inoculation Return	A.D.M.S.

1875 Wt. W593/826 1,000,000 4/15 J.B.C. & A. A.D.S.S./Forms/C. 2118.

Army Form C. 2118

WAR DIARY
or
INTELLIGENCE SUMMARY
(Erase heading not required.)

Instructions regarding War Diaries and Intelligence Summaries are contained in F. S. Regs., Part II. and the Staff Manual respectively. Title Pages will be prepared in manuscript.

Place	Date	Hour	Summary of Events and Information	Remarks and references to Appendices
27.X.17.23. BAILLEUL	19/6		Continued	
			Monthly Sar-Ret	To Whom Subject
			War Diary	D.A.G Base via A.D.M.S.
			Cash a/c AFN1531a.	Base Cashier
		"	Officers Allowance Claim A.A. P1734a.	Base Cashier
	20/6		Field ambulance sports. Route march in the morning	
	21/6		Route march & football & cricket in afternoon. Lieut. E. Cameron R.A.M.C. Res. proceeded to Pont Remy as Billeting Officer.	
	22/6		The three motor ambulances remaining will be returned tomorrow. Motor Cyclers + Drivers returned today.	
	23/6		All ambulance equipment packed ready for the road	Hut
	25/6		Have left 27.X.11.C.S.S. and entrained at BAILLEUL MAIN. Arrived at MAIN at 8-40 p.m. and were all entrained at 10 p.m.	

1875 Wt. W593/826 1,000,000 4/15 J.B.C. & A. A.D.S.S./Forms/C. 2118.

WAR DIARY
or
INTELLIGENCE SUMMARY

(Erase heading not required.)

Army Form C. 2118

Instructions regarding War Diaries and Intelligence Summaries are contained in F. S. Regs., Part II. and the Staff Manual respectively. Title Pages will be prepared in manuscript.

Place	Date	Hour	Summary of Events and Information	Remarks and references to Appendices
B TRAIN			Each train consisted of 1 Officers carriage 14 flat trucks, 33 covered trucks. Each flat truck trees 4 axles. Each covered truck twenty two 6 H.D. or 7 D. axles or 40 men.	Hut
LONGPRES	24/6		Arrived at LONGPRES 7-40 p.m. Commenced to detrain 9-30. Completed detraining at 11-30 p.m. The delay was due to an A.S.C. Coy. detraining at the same time, and being unable to move the train to facilitate matters.	Hut
ERQNIES	25/6		Marched at or 12 midnight and arrived at ERQNIES. [MAP II (LENS).] Reft. detour owing to at 3-30 A.M.	nyst
"	26/6		Spent the day resting and arranging billets. Three fried racks and two cradles on the limber wagons in order to carry 30 or 40 rolled tins for extra drinking water. Les training commenced today in our Brigade area - C. Section under command of Capt. H.S. Curell are ordered to Lieuts. Bluck & Gillespie with Brigade proceeded to cooperate with Sgt. 10th R.W.K. Regt. by forming a M.D.S. and an A.D.S.	nyst

1875 Wt. W593/826 1,000,000 4/15 J.B.C. & A. A.D.S.S./Forms/C.2118.

WAR DIARY
or
INTELLIGENCE SUMMARY

(Erase heading not required.)

Army Form C. 2118

Place	Date	Hour	Summary of Events and Information	Remarks and references to Appendices
ERQNIES	24/16		Sent in a Programme for the week, to-day, to the A.D.M.S. Church Parade 9-55. No. 21499 21 Cpl. H.C. Anderson M.T. returned to OC 40/12 F.A. Bde; on case of cerebro-spinal fever transferred to 39 C.C.S. ALLONVILLE.	Her.
"	28/16		Field Training, and a Route march	Mor.
"	29/16		a Divisional Field day for the 3 Field Ambulances. The Pioneer Battalion representing the fighting force of Troops. 650 casualties passed through by A.? C.C.S.º (supposed) D.C.S. and an O.S.? which 141 passed through an Fueld Ambulance. Capt. T.T. CORKILL was an charge of the Bearer Sub-Divisions. Capt J.O. SHELDON in charge D.C.S. and myself in charge of M.D.S.	Mor.
"	30/16		a Brigade Field day Capt. R.J Jaffrey W.R. section attached to 20 Bn. R.J. in the morning & to the 2½ Middlesex in afternoon. Capt. T.T. CORKILL W.C. Section attached to 11/12 R.W.S. in the morning and to the 10 R.W.K. in the afternoon.	Mor.

WAR DIARY
or
INTELLIGENCE SUMMARY
(Erase heading not required.)

Army Form C. 2118

Place	Date	Hour	Summary of Events and Information	Remarks and references to Appendices
ERQUINGHEM	31/8		Owing to the constant rain yesterday the Divisional full-dress inspection by the General has been postponed till the 4th inst. All our Field Ambulance personnel have been told all spare clothing divisible to-day to account for the number of lice which seem to have come from the dormers on which they are sleeping. Capt. R. L. IMPEY has proceeded to HYDE PARK CORNER by motor in order to attend a General Court Martial throughout the month. He has been only a few our days. Major came in. O.C. 135th W. ( ) Ambulance.	4/8
			August 31st 1916.	

War Diary
of
129th 3rd Bah
List Surgeon
for
1/4/16 to 30/9/16

(Volume V)

COMMITTEE FOR THE
MEDICAL HISTORY OF THE WAR
Date -9 DEC. 1916

Army Form C. 2118

Vol VI SEPT. 1916.
WAR DIARY or INTELLIGENCE SUMMARY
(Erase heading not required.)

Place	Date	Hour	Summary of Events and Information	Remarks and references to Appendices
ERQUIÈRES	1/9/16		Field day according to Programme arranged —	Appx.
"	2/9/16		Monsieur M. MARRIE (Armed Interpreter) reported his arrival on 21/8/16.	Appx.
"	3/9/16		Church Parade 9 – 30 am. Have 2 hour in the afternoon.	Appx.
"	4/9/16		Field day for the Field Ambulances. Returned early on account of rate called away.	Appx.
BECORDEL	5/9/16		139 M.T. of A.T. transport arrived of reinforcements for a camp for 62D BECORDEL – BECOUR (Map 62D E 19.1.1.) at 10 – 30 am and arrived at E 12.11 on the 6th.	Appx.
"	6/16		Remainder of Field Ambulance arrived by road to LONGPRES stn. and entrained there for MERICOURT and from there marched to our new camp joining the Transport, arriving about 10 p.m.	Appx.
"			LIEUT. D.P.T. Rennes was directed to relieve Capt. Scott M.O. 4/R 10½ R.W.K. today. Capt. Scott has been associated with Infantry and allotted the Relief. Took place on the 21st August 1916.	
"	7/9/16		Day spent in arrange up camp, and improving the sanitation. A new water supply commenced & 9th & XV Corps. MAP.REF. 62D 12. a.1.1. E	Appx.
"	8/9/16		Lieut. T.W. Sheldon R.A.M.C. has been detailed to report with C. Tent-sub-division to O.C. Corps Main Dressing Station for temporary duty.	Appx.
"	9/9/16		Moved to 62 D.F. 4.d.6.7. with the Brigade before moving into position.	Appx.

Lieut T.W. SHELDON has been attached with C. Tent sub-div. to XV. Corps Rest station.

WAR DIARY
or
INTELLIGENCE SUMMARY

(Erase heading not required.)

Army Form C. 2118

Instructions regarding War Diaries and Intelligence Summaries are contained in F.S. Regs., Part II. and the Staff Manual respectively. Title Pages will be prepared in manuscript.

Place	Date	Hour	Summary of Events and Information	Remarks and references to Appendices
27/IX/33 BAILLEUL	15/6		Continued	
			DAILY contin. SUBJECT To whom	
			When Necessary.	
			Names of officers & others granted Special Leave — A.D.M.S.	
			Returns of Courts Martial — A.D.M.S.	
			Chronic Disease Return (Albuminuria, Nephritis & Dropsy) — A.D.M.S.	
			Reinforcement Return — A.D.M.S.	
			QUARTERLY	
			Kit issued to prisoners return of Cost. — A.D.M.S.	

WAR DIARY or INTELLIGENCE SUMMARY

Army Form C. 2118

Place	Date	Hour	Summary of Events and Information	Remarks and references to Appendices
BECORDEL	9/7/16		HQrs moved to 62.D.7.T.6.3.3. in the XV Corps Collecting Station for Walking Wounded. Capt. T.W. Coxwell and Lieut. D.P. Thomas left this evening for the Div.s. Collecting Station under Major Williamson.	Hut.
"	10/7/16		Took over Corps Collecting station from 1/2 end Wood at 6 a.m. Capt. Rowbottom R.A.M.C. & the 140 O.R. — for W.W. Have sent one motor cyclist to Major Williamson for duty. Have sent Lieut. T.C. Cameron with B + C. Reserves to report to O.C. Division C.S. this afternoon, also Capt. R.W. Hogg with 54 NCO & men (Reserves) which includes A. Section Bearers. Lieut + 60 men Ayrs R.A.M.C. reports for duty on the 9/12 inst.	Hut.
"	10/7/16		Have handed over charge of the Corps Collecting Stn. for W.W. 6 Col. O'Neill O.C. No 1 N.Z. Field Ambulance, who have joined up with my H.Q. Sent 60 NCO + men & 140 O. M.A. + 33 NCO + men & the 13 Bn Y.C. forward to O.C. Div.s. Collecting Station. All my Bearers have returned for rest, along with Capt. T.F. Coxwell and Lieut. D.P. Thomas. A second entry + start to their camp is in progress and also a large hut for attending to the walking wounded as they enter.	Hut.

WAR DIARY
or
INTELLIGENCE SUMMARY

(Erase heading not required.)

Army Form C. 2118

Instructions regarding War Diaries and Intelligence Summaries are contained in F. S. Regs., Part II. and the Staff Manual respectively. Title Pages will be prepared in manuscript.

Place	Date	Hour	Summary of Events and Information	Remarks and references to Appendices
"	13/9/16		Have endorsed on at ambulance stands considerably a wearing place with a large wet tent. RAMC has also been expected. Capt. T. T. Cowell and Lieut. J. G. Thomas with 30 bearers proceeded this afternoon to O.C. 138 F.A. at MAMETZ.	Htd.
"	14/9/16		Lieut. C. Cameron with all the remaining bearers proceeded to take over a M.D. Collecting Station this morning in order to be in position by 11 p.m. on 14th. Very heavy artillery giving commenced this evening at 6 p.m. and continued all night.	Htd.
"	15/9/16		Several quiet as regards casualties, but at 10 a.m. at the Advanced Dressing Room were kept hard at it all day + night. Over 2000 Canad. making the came through. Several more wounded. Seven m.o. were kept hard at it and the C.C.S. before 12 midnight. Our Division has been will. men at OS.H. and the C.E.S.	
"	16/9/16	6 a.m.	Advanced + captured FLEURS before midday. Huns were temp. checked. All wounded (except 30 stretcher) were got in with the British. The prisoners, still continues short, and many wounded being first under gone. Walking cases been a large diment for stretchers + blankets. There has been a large diment for stretchers + blankets at the speed for assessing what the C.C. I can supply.	Htd.

1875 Wt. W593/826 1,000,000 4/15 J.B.C. & A. A.D.S.S./Forms/C. 2118.

WAR DIARY
or
INTELLIGENCE SUMMARY

Army Form C. 2118

Place	Date	Hour	Summary of Events and Information	Remarks and references to Appendices
"	16/7/6		The char-a-banes placed at the disposal of this one. corps. C.S. were of great value, both in evacuating wounded from the front line and in sending relief parties of bearers to get front. These char-a-banes kept on fall of MONTAUBAN & the SHRINE. Battle still a continuous hum with guns going.	Mor.
"	14/6		Orders were recd. on on division 54th from & R.A.P. on to advance. Officers were sent forward to reconnoitre & settle and advanced site. It. Regt. had been sitting in touch with the amo. up & advanced Dressing Stations Road. the Bearer Divisions were used to evacuate wounded from the R.A.P.'s to advanced Dressing Posts and from Main to A.D.S.	Arr.
"			Our A.D.2.D.T. Lt. G navy-we joined by our Tent Sub. Division and bearers under a M.O. under a M.O. and A.R.P. formed by bearers joined by 2 Tent Sub. Division under O.C. of 135 F.A.	not

1875 Wt. W593/826 1,000,000 4/15 J.B.C. & A. A.D.S.S./Forms/C. 2118.

Army Form C. 2118

WAR DIARY
or
INTELLIGENCE SUMMARY
(Erase heading not required.)

Place	Date	Hour	Summary of Events and Information	Remarks and references to Appendices
			The following is the initial arrangement for working the Corps COLLECTING STATION except where a big engagement is on, when all the staff is working any hr and day with only a few hours rest per diem. Each of 7 takes a turn of 24 hours and arranges for a day and night staff of Officers, NCOs, and dressers as follows:	Ack.

BY DAY   For A + D Room   2 NCOs +   1 Pte
            for Rest Stn   —   1 Pte

BY NIGHT   For A + D Room   1 NCO +   1 Pte
            for Base Stn   —   1 Pte

Dressing Room.

BY DAY   Medical Officers   2   1
            Nursing Orderlies   1 NCO +   4 Ptes
            Supervising & Inoculation Clerk   1 NCO +   4 Ptes
            This NCO also compiles a nominal roll of all wounded for Office C.R.S.

BY NIGHT   Medical Officer   1   —
            Nursing Orderlies   —   4 Ptes
            Supervising & Inoculation Clerk   1 NCO.   —

WAR DIARY or INTELLIGENCE SUMMARY

Army Form C. 2118

(Erase heading not required.)

Place	Date	Hour	Summary of Events and Information	Remarks and references to Appendices
			On cases being admitted full particulars are taken at the Y.M.C. (A.F.W. 3118) and Tuft Slip (A.F.W. 3210) are compiled from the following & patients, with exception of the diagnosis. The Medical Officer examines, writes diagnosis on the Y.M.C. & T.S. The designation of "patient" and diagnosis. The wounds are now regarded as required above all considered fit for duty with trivial wounds or slightly wounded sick buts slip and cases "return to duty", on the Y.M.C. and parts or men "to the M.M.P." in camp. All others, on retaining him till the morning for the M.M.P. In all cases of wounded M.O. orders A.T.S. on the Y.M.C & on a large T.T. on the lines of that dealt with on Y.M.C. serum has been given. The following & Evacuation clerk then arranges for transfer in a motor ambulance of cases — a frame to Nurses or C.R.S. with the patient has had a hot bowl of soup, coffee or tea with what comforts such as bread & butter, biscuit, cigarettes. These comforts are now given in a waiting room just before the M.O. sees him in the dressing room along side. This process of evacuation takes on an average for each patient one and a quarter minutes. On patients leaving here the pack stored waiting room all ammunition & government kit is collected by us and sent .... dump hides	Mil

Army Form C. 2118.

WAR DIARY
or
INTELLIGENCE SUMMARY.
(Erase heading not required.)

Instructions regarding War Diaries and Intelligence Summaries are contained in F. S. Regs., Part II. and the Staff Manual respectively. Title pages will be prepared in manuscript.

Place	Date	Hour	Summary of Events and Information	Remarks and references to Appendices
			Strain noon on Oct 16th till Noon on Oct 14th 4506 Wounded Gas through Gas. 2930 to C.C.S. 1008 to July 568 to C.C.S.	
			The following are the casualties which occurred in my S.A. on Oct 15th & 16th	
			Pte Stevens W.H. SHELL SHOCK C.C.S.	
			" Warrin " " " C.R.S.	Hut
			" Seaman J " " " C.R.S.	
			" S Elliott Wound C.C.S.	
			L/Cpl White SHELL SHOCK C.C.S.	
			L/Cpl Bailey " " C.R.S.	
			Pte James D " " C.R.S.	
			Pte d'Cora Wound C.C.S.	
			All my officers non-commissioned officers and men worked with great smartness and efficiency and at any day during these operations and did not spare themselves in the least, well	

WAR DIARY
or
INTELLIGENCE SUMMARY.
(Erase heading not required.)

Army Form C. 2118.

Place	Date	Hour	Summary of Events and Information	Remarks and references to Appendices
			recognizing the importance of their duties. Sergt. Coney who was in charge of the 4th Bomb Reserves issued munitions as required. His devotion to duty, the coolness continued during the whole of the operations and displayed exactly to prevent any confusion.	Cont.

Army Form C. 2118

WAR DIARY
or
INTELLIGENCE SUMMARY
(Erase heading not required.)

Instructions regarding War Diaries and Intelligence Summaries are contained in F.S. Regs., Part II. and the Staff Manual respectively. Title Pages will be prepared in manuscript.

Place	Date	Hour	Summary of Events and Information	Remarks and references to Appendices
"	18/9/16		Thin feed of the line recently taken has been maintained. Capt. H.T. Cowell arrived back at 9-30 A.M. with the Bearer division also Lieut. S.R. Thomas. In the afternoon Lieut. B. Wilson arrived back.	Appx
"	19/9/16		Consolidating the line still continues.	Appx
"	20/9/16		Capt. R.S. Jackson, Lieut. W.S. Dixon & R. Young with Bearer division proceeded to the Quarry at 9-45 am to support 2/C (?) 2/C (?) EAST LANCS 2. FIELD AMBULANCE on duty. Young & Capt. R.P. J. Flemming were wounded & sent to C.R.S.	Appx
"	21/9/16		Capt. R.J. Gourlay, R.J. Todd & S. Dixon with bearers returned today for rest. C.P. Willis. Lieut. A.O.M.S. Lieut. R.S. Todd, D.S.Y. Renwar & Duff with 3 NCO's and 20 men proceeded to HEILLY to review a similar number of Amb. continued till etc. Heavy rain commenced on the 14/9/16 and continues.	Appx

1875 Wt. W593/826 1,000,000 4/15 J.B.C. & A. A.D.S.S./Forms/C. 2118.

WAR DIARY
INTELLIGENCE SUMMARY
(Erase heading not required.)

Army Form C. 2118

Place	Date	Hour	Summary of Events and Information	Remarks and references to Appendices
"	22/9/16		Operations of matters advance continues	Above.
"	23/9/16		"	
"	24/9/16		"	Above.
"	25/9/16		Attack commenced at about 12 noon to-day. 9th Divisions now in action, of XV Corps on 55th, 21st and Highland Divs. With 9th 41st 33rd 12th Divisions, and their S. Lister Cavalry in reserve.	Above.
			From 12 Noon a very steady stream of wounded came in and continued till 4 A.m. on 26th.	Above.
			By order from the A.D.M.S. 41st Division dated 25/9/16 9 Rank detailed Capt. P. J. Dankey with 61 NCO's men of the Bearer Division to report to O.C. 64/2 Field Ambulance at 6 AM at the A.D.S. BERNAFEY WOOD. Also Capt. J.W. Rubbon has been detailed to report to 18 H 42 Infy B.de. headquarters near E on a.q. on temp. charge of 26/2 Royal Fusiliers.	
	26/9/16		From 12 Noon yesterday to 12 Noon to-day 1616 wounded have passed through here. Capt Duffy & Bearers are now collecting wounded [illegible] GAUDICOURT and being [illegible] back a 4 mile carry. Several hundred prisoners taken this morning	Above.

Army Form C. 2118.

WAR DIARY
or
INTELLIGENCE SUMMARY.
(Erase heading not required.)

Instructions regarding War Diaries and Intelligence Summaries are contained in F.S. Regs., Part II. and the Staff Manual respectively. Title pages will be prepared in manuscript.

Place	Date	Hour	Summary of Events and Information	Remarks and references to Appendices
"	24/9/16		Battle still continues but will be no casualties from 12 noon yesterday to 12 noon today 495 casualties. General Strength.	ffwd
"	25/9/16		No casualties. General Strength up to 12 noon today. Officers A.D.M.S. has placed any A.A. at the disposal of the 112 Division.	ffwd
			From tonight my unit has been placed at the disposal of the A.D.M.S. of the 21 Division. I shall relieve a A.A. of the 55 Div. the relief to be completed by 8 am. 29 Sept. The 55 Div. A.A. has an A.D.S. at the shrine & another at the Quarry. Details as to the time of march & interval of your unit will be issued later. Signed G.W. Parker Col. A.D.M.S. 5.45 p.m.	
SHRINE & QUARRY.	29/9/16		Relief completed at 8 a.m. and a report sent to A.D.M.S. 21 Divn. The Quarry has been made into a Rest station for any A.A. on return from the Reserve Dumps + A.D.S. Capt. R.J. Gostey has proceeded with 20 of the Reserve to relieve	ffwd

T2134. Wt. W708—776. 500000. 4/15. Sir J. C. & S.

WAR DIARY or INTELLIGENCE SUMMARY

Army Form C. 2118.

Place	Date	Hour	Summary of Events and Information	Remarks and references to Appendices
?			Stretcher bearers of the 5/Divis. S.A. on the road to FLEURS and will work up to 6 p.m. Capt. J. on Brown is placed in charge of the A.D.S. till 6 p.m.	then
			The following is the arrangement at the A.D.S. SHRINE DUMPS — the bearers are divided into two parties of 36 by day & 36 by night from 7 a.m. to 7 p.m. & 7 p.m. to 7 a.m. with one officer each shift. There are 3 dumps in connection with the 3 R.A.P. & 12 bearers at each Dump. The medical officer supervises the running of these Dumps.	
			The SHRINE A.D.S. has a personnel of 10 — one sergt. gen. duty 1 clerk 2 Receivers at the entrance to receive wounded 2 Dressers 1 officer in charge of officer on duty 1 Cook & 2 bearers at teur sub Bris.	
			During the day a fairly constant stream of wounded passed through. Capt. R.J. Per Burgeaud his duties unflinchingly along with Receivers are kept busy all day under a constant hail of Shell fire.	

WAR DIARY
or
INTELLIGENCE SUMMARY.
(Erase heading not required.)

Army Form C. 2118.

Place	Date	Hour	Summary of Events and Information	Remarks and references to Appendices
	9/30		Last night Lieut W.T. Wilson and Capt. J.T. Cowell went out to A.D.S. where were a good many casualties passing through their hands all night. Shelling was heavy during the night. We read from LONGUEVAL to FLEURS (GUARDS) causing many casualties amongst the transport. All day long a fairly constant flow of wounded came in.	Hut
	10		41 Division In 12 noon Sept 31st. Officers killed wounded missing 2 6 Other Ranks 32 132 — Evacuated Sick 351. Recommended for military cross Capt. Thomas T. Cowell S.R. " " " Capt. R.L. Tomkey S.R. " " " Lieut. S.C. Thomas " " " Lieut W.T. Wilson Mentioned in dispatches Capt. & Lt. Dunn C.F. " " " " Capt. J. Thomas C.F.	S.R. Hut

Recommended for military conduct
Sergt. Palmer, Gammon, and Orton —
Recommended for mention in dispatches
Q'mast Sergt. Holmes, Sergt. S. Roney, Pte Newman, Pte Stone
Pte Tilley, Pte Aerhurst, Pte Young, Pte Moore, Pte Price,
Pte Savage, Pte Reynolds, Pte Leigh, & Lemming.
Officers wounded & remain
Lieutenant Mathers. Pte Hill Hope. Lance Cpl Spencer
Cpl Hardock. Pte Almer

"He did" Capt X. For constant devotion to duty in a conspicuous
manner while leading his men night and day through heavy
shell fire. Intellect wounded, this evinces gallantry & Exhibition
gave great confidence to his bearers who were more
by him many times.

WAR DIARY
or
INTELLIGENCE SUMMARY.
(Erase heading not required.)

Army Form C. 2118.

Place	Date	Hour	Summary of Events and Information	Remarks and references to Appendices
			The[?] vigilance[?] needed[?] the great coolness and devotion to duty which during this time under heavy shell fire on dressing stations[?]	
			mention in dispatches — for Officers — for constant devotion to duty on many occasions and under heavy shell fire, while dressing the wounded	Capt.
"			mention in dispatches — for men + N.C.O.'s — for constant devotion to duty which was performed often under a certain amount of shell fire.	
			Oct. 1st 1916.	
			[signature] Major [?]	
			O.C. 139 Yeo[?] Ambulance.	

War Diary

139th Field Amb.

October 1916

SHEET 1

Army Form C. 2118.

VOL VI 1916

SEPTEMBER WAR DIARY
or
INTELLIGENCE SUMMARY.
(Erase heading not required.)

Instructions regarding War Diaries and Intelligence Summaries are contained in F. S. Regs., Part II. and the Staff Manual respectively. Title pages will be prepared in manuscript.

Place	Date	Hour	Summary of Events and Information	Remarks and references to Appendices
	1/9/16		The advanced dressing station was shelled constantly Yesterday all day but there has been no direct hit. One shell close by accounted for 2 killed and 13 wounded. A.F.W. 3121 (Honours & Rewards) forwarded to day to H.Q. with the names of officers, NCO's & men recommended for exceptional good work during the past four months. Last night Lt Capt H Coveill with bearers up the line & Lt Wilson at at Shrine.	Oken
	2/9/16		To day Capt. R.H. Imery up the line & Capt Mr. H Nunn at the Shrine — a slow stream of casualties with a rush of about 3 hours in the afternoon. Last night Lt Wilson up the line & Capt Coveill at the SHRINE. During the night two of our bearers were wounded but and his for slight shock but got battle wounds to carry on. 2 R.O.s to call on the 6th & 7th for a squad of 6. to replace those cracked out at FLEURS.	

WAR DIARY
or
INTELLIGENCE SUMMARY.

Army Form C. 2118.

SEPT. 1916

Date	Hour	Summary of Events and Information	Remarks and references to Appendices
2/10		The 21 Division was relieved by the 12 Division this morning. Our Reserve + Capt Carlisle + the Division returned to Quarry for rest. The Huns counter-attacked most deliberately putting a tremendous shell our Quarry and managed to get in our support line but only succeeded in wounding one man within a few yards of me and I entered the Quarry. WAR DIARY sent off today.	over
3/10		By orders from the A.D.M.S. 41 Division I have arrived with my H.A. at FLATIRON COPSE ready to take over from No 2 NZ Field Ambulance and at the same time relieving a rest camp used by my four officers and men who have written here in relation to his different occasions. By orders from the A.D.M.S. I Capt E.J. Skidden has been placed in temporary charge of 26th R.T. on the 25th Sept. and Lieut W.H. Allen temporary in charge of 12 East Surrey & Lieut. CAMERON R.A.F.	Ant

WAR DIARY
INTELLIGENCE SUMMARY
(Erase heading not required.)

Army Form C. 2118.

Place	Date	Hour	Summary of Events and Information	Remarks and references to Appendices
	3/2		I have sent Capt. A.C. Sargay & 2 Lt. Wilson up the line to adjust our dispositions and get familiar with the working of the present S.A.	Capt
			I have applied for 4 officers + 65 other ranks as I am deficient of this number — 3 officers + 23 other ranks one at 3 C.C.S. and 1 N.C.O. + 14 N.C.O.s down and one at the C.R.S. exclusive of the details for short of one officer + 24 other ranks viz Lt. CAMERON SICK.	
			LIEUT W.F. WILSON placed in (temporary) charge of the 12th EAST SURREY. I have detailed 2nd Lt. Davis and 45 other ranks of the 140th A. to proceed to THISTLE ALLEY at 8 p.m. in order to relieve my stretcher already up on the morning. I have ambulance wagons & rations for 24 hours. On their ambulance wagon of the 140th placed at my disposal tonight, at 4 p.m. we take over the running of its relieving Post and at 9 p.m. had our orderly Post and advances moving.	Hest

WAR DIARY or INTELLIGENCE SUMMARY

Army Form C. 2118.

Place	Date	Hour	Summary of Events and Information	Remarks and references to Appendices
	4/6		Last night was exceptionally quiet, all the New Zealand Bearers were relieved before 4 am & every thing evacuated. Rain had ceased & having made the ambulance Care & out more horse ambulance useful on at my disposal today from the 140 FA A.F.TODD, THOMAS & DUFF with 2 NCOs & 20 men rejoined Corps. Inspected my lorry wir this morning and attached a copy of one created made out for running the strain between the Regimental aid Posts & the 3rd gun cap.	
			Capt. T. McCRIRICK R.A.M.C. reported to me for duty today. 14 REINFORCEMENTS arrived today. 5 of these 9 have sent up the line tonight & the remainder will follow at 7 A.M. on the 5/12 I have applied to have Lieut. Wilson replaced by Capt Jim Brown. I have arranged for our water cart full to proceed to THISTLE DUMP twice daily morn. & even.	
	5/6		My BEARERS under Capt. H. Carrill went into the line this morning for 24 hours, while the 140 FA remainder in reserve at THISTLE ALLEY.	

WAR DIARY
or
INTELLIGENCE SUMMARY.
(Erase heading not required.)

Army Form C. 2118.

Place	Date	Hour	Summary of Events and Information	Remarks and references to Appendices
	5/10/16		continued. under Lieut. Davis of same ambulance. I sent Capt. J.M. Brown to THISTLE ALLEY this morning to relieve Lieut. DAVIS. and afterwards Lieut R.T. TODD to relieve Capt. Brown who has been detailed forthwith to take over medical charge of the 10/19 R.W. Surrey Regt. in place of Lieut. FULLER Died. Our Division has got into the line with very few casualties. There has been a fairly steady stream of wounded passing all last night & to-day. By order from A.D.M.S. by signal S.221 Capt. BROWN has now been detailed to proceed to take over medical charge of 190th Brigade R.F.A. at POMIERS REDOUBT. The 139th F.A. under Capt. Coweill have been relieved this morning by the 135th F.A. under Capt. Kinney, the 139 remaining in reserve at THISTLE ALLEY. for Governor's stunt.	
	6/10/16		This morning I arrived THISTLE ALLEY & McCORMIC'S POST. much shelling going on #0 within 200 yards of the latter on its left. Capt. M.C. CRIRIE U/o at THISTLE ALLEY.	

Place	Date	Hour	Summary of Events and Information	Remarks and references to Appendices
	10/6/16		I gave out my defence for duration commencing on the 4th October. All the Officers and Bearers, motor ambulances and horse ambulance wagons of the 3rd Field Ambulance LESS two Officers (OC & one other) of the 138 & 140 1/2 F.A. 2 motor ambulances of 140 1/2 + 5 Motor Ambulances of 135 2 F.A. and 3 Horse amb. wagons of 140 1/2 F.A. Besides the above I had 2 N.C.O. + 30 men from each Inf. Bde. to work with the bearers. Also 1 NCO Inf. Clerks – two Runs + 2 at THISTLE ALLEY. Situation of R.A.P. for tomorrow Capt. Langan 15/19 HANTS 122 Bde NORTH ROAD 200 yds to left of Lieut. Williamson 32 Royal Fus. 124 Bde TURK LANE M 30 6.5.4. Lieut. W.T. Wilson 12 East Lancs. M 30 t 7.2 Lieut. Hart 21/2 K.R.R. 124 Bde on side Trench of TURK LANE Capt. Fuller 10/2 Queens 124 " M 30 d 4.4 Capt. Hodgson 26/2 Royal Fus.124 "	

WAR DIARY
or
INTELLIGENCE SUMMARY.
(Erase heading not required.)

Army Form C. 2118.

Place	Date	Hour	Summary of Events and Information	Remarks and references to Appendices
	6/9/16		Capt Elliott 16th K.R.R. 122 R.Be. M36 b 7.4 probably morning	
			Lieut Tray 11 R.W. Kent 122 R.Be. M26 a 2.5 "	
			Lieut Brown 190th R.F.A. Bde. to McCORMICKS POST	
			"	
			The following on the operation order issued by me	
			in conjunction with operation order issued by A.D.M.S. 41st	
			Div.	
			Stretcher bearers of 138th field ambulance with 32 infantry bearers	
			will be in reserve at MEDICAL DUMP from 12 Noon on Wed 4/12 inst.	
			140 M.A. bearers and 32 Inf. bearers attached to be at	
			THISTLE ALLEY at 5-30 a.m. on 4/12 inst in charge of Capt.	
			ROWBOTHOM to be ready to proceed to McCORMICK POST.	
			129th F.A. bearers and 32 Inf. bearers attached to be at	
			THISTLE ALLEY at the same time 5-30 a.m. on 4/12 inst. ½	
			of Lieut TODD ready to proceed to McCORMICKS POST.	

WAR DIARY
or
INTELLIGENCE SUMMARY.
(Erase heading not required.)

Army Form C. 2118.

Place	Date	Hour	Summary of Events and Information	Remarks and references to Appendices
	6/9/16		The Officer i/c Bearer Division (Capt. Rowbottom) will send forward at once 3 squads of 4 bearers each to each R.A.P. These (3) squads of 4 bearers each for each R.A.P. will be in reserve at McCormic's Post. All (2) above squads are to work only between the R.A.P's & McCormic's Post. The remainder of the bearers will work between the McCormic's Post & Thistle Alley. On no account must more than 2 inf. bearers be with any stretcher squad. Only cases requiring prompt & urgent treatment will be bound. Every endeavour will be made for a speedy evacuation. The O.C. Bearers if requiring more bearers will ring a telephone message to A.D.M.S. via H.Q. 124 Inf. Bde. Any casualties amongst personnel will be reported at once to me.	

Army Form C. 2118.

WAR DIARY
or
INTELLIGENCE SUMMARY.
(Erase heading not required.)

Place	Date	Hour	Summary of Events and Information	Remarks and references to Appendices
	6/7/16		All bearers must carry one water proof sheet, one water bottle full, one iron ration and a haltz for 24 hrs.	
			Capt. Corkill will be in command at THISTLE ALLEY assisted by Lieut. B.T. Thomas	
			The following Officers are detailed for duty at FLAT IRON COPSE Capt. R.S. Sampey, Lieut. Roch & Lieut. Duff	
	7/7/16		All very quiet this morning and up to 1-45 when Zero Hour commenced and our guns opened forth a number so intense as to be beyond description. When our infantry advanced to the attack, but were only able to obtain their first objective. The machine gun cross fire was so terrific and caused many casualties. Bombardment began to slow in about 5 p.m. and gradually increased in numbers. At 7-30 I had to send off 6 char-à-bancs and 6 motor ambulance cars. Capt. SHELDON R.A.M.C. no. 26/17 R.T. has reported sick with gastritis + is in a serious condition & to VII C.C.S. for W.W.	

T.134. Wt. W708—776. 500000. 4/15. Sir J. C. & S.

WAR DIARY or INTELLIGENCE SUMMARY

Army Form C. 2118.

Place	Date	Hour	Summary of Events and Information	Remarks and references to Appendices
	7/9/16		Lieut Leep of 9th 11th R.W. Kents has been wounded this afternoon in the attack & Guinness. He walked into McCormic's Post as cheery as a lark. The day before his R.A.P. was blown in. At about 10 p.m. the O.C. 9 S.M.L. & Major H-a-Court (Staff officer Div.) arrived with a report that many wounded of the 12th Rile were still lying out + in the trenches. I escorted him to McCormic's Post and we found that many stretcher bearers were working smartly and were being given stimulants to clear the stew remaining at the R.A.P. To make sure of this I went and visited the R.A.P. and sent the following report to the A.D.M.S. during the night after leaving Major Shuttleworth & Major H-a-Court visited the following R.A.P.s M20.6.54 M30.6.7.2 & M30.d.7.4 and found the evacuation in full swing M30.6.54 had only one wounded man at 2 p.m. M30 d.7.2 Bde arm and M30.d.7.4 had two ready for evacuation. The excess of casualties at this time was due to all the bearers (ambulance + infantry) being tried out, as far as I could gather there	

WAR DIARY
or
INTELLIGENCE SUMMARY.
(Erase heading not required.)

Army Form C. 2118.

Place	Date	Hour	Summary of Events and Information	Remarks and references to Appendices
	9/9/16		appears to be a good many wounded on the front line. They were about 150 cases in TURK LANE on their way from R.A.P. to THISTLE ALLEY. No congestion whatever. The CORMIC'S POST was kept very busy all day and all N.	
	10/9/16	6 A.M.	At 6 A.M. the 13th F.A. arrived at McCORMIC'S POST to relieve the bearers of the 139½ + 140½ F.A. + Infantry attached who will proceed to MEDICAL DUMP for rest which is urgently needed. Lieut. ROCH has relieved Capt. ROWBOTHAM + Lieut. TODD at McCORMIC'S POST. Lieut. DUFF has proceeded to THISTLE ALLEY to relieve Capt. CORKILL at 7 A.M. Capt. HOGG takes another party of Infantry up at noon today. I have been major Livingston on my return at 7 A.M. and recommended to him a system of reliefs of Infantry bearers from the front line to ABBEY ROAD, and of AMBULANCE BEARERS and Infantry attached from ABBEY ROAD to THISTLE ALLEY.	his

T.J.134. Wt. W708-776. 500000. 4/15. Sir J. C. & S.

WAR DIARY or INTELLIGENCE SUMMARY

Army Form C. 2118.

Place	Date	Hour	Summary of Events and Information	Remarks and references to Appendices
	5/10/16		continued. Capt VICKERS reported him for duty at 8 p.m. for night duty. Capt BINNY is to be at THISTLE ALLEY to take charge of 100 Inf Bearers & get in touch with Lieut. ROCH at McCORMIES POST and work in conjunction with him at 8 p.m. Lieut. ROCH will return to rest with his Section when relieved at 8 p.m. on the 9th. Capt Loudon & Hott proceeded to the front on the 9th. Capt BINNY will be relieved at McCORMIES POST by Lieut DAVIS and bearers of the 140 F.A. & Inf. attached. Lieut CONOLLY will relieve Lieut. DUFF at 9 a.m. on the 9/12. The number of wounded from 12 Noon on the 9/12 till 12 Noon 13 Oct which passed through my A.D.S. FLAT IRON COPSE was 23 officers and 563 other ranks. Orders 240 from A.D.M.S. 41 Div. to recall all Infantry bearers at once. Lieut WOGG THISTLE ALLY & McCORMIES POINT at	

WAR DIARY
or
INTELLIGENCE SUMMARY
(Erase heading not required.)

Army Form C. 2118.

13

Place	Date	Hour	Summary of Events and Information	Remarks and references to Appendices
	8/9/16		men in general, and ordered to return to their Transport lines. Guides from A.D.M.S. guides were detailed to proceed to COUGHDROP and met casualties to the CORMIES POINT and to entrust stretcher squads to COUGHDROP A.D.S. of 5 LONDON T.A. for care of the 41st Division that were Bare Stretcher. By order from the A.D.M.S. Capt McCRIRICK proceeded this afternoon to report himself to O.C. 11 R.W. Kent Regt. in place of Lieut Facey wounded. The day has been spent in strengthening the station guard.	
	9/9/16		Mule bearers of 140½ T.A. relieved the 138½ T.A. at 2 p.m. and the 139½ T.A. relieved the 140½ at 11 p.m. Lieut THOMAS is in charge of the 139½. Lieut DAVIS from A.D.M.S. POPPY reports that a considerable number of wounded in POPPY'S trench about N19 k 26 require clearing please take immediate action. (A.D.M.S No S 250) to clear four line of Stretcher. (A.D.M.S.No S 245)	✓

WAR DIARY
or
INTELLIGENCE SUMMARY.
(Erase heading not required.)

Army Form C. 2118.

Place	Date	Hour	Summary of Events and Information	Remarks and references to Appendices
	9/10/16		Steps were immediately taken, and 9 sub. Capt. Jon Jury sent forward to see that graph state were taken. On his return he reported that a state considerable number of wounded of that 6 is Jewel's was turned out to be 12. Reserves were at once sent forward to clear state. SBs only available wounded supported by En OC. at this time were 6 of 4th R.A.P. of yr 3/2nd R. Sus. and 6 at the R.A.P. of 10th R.W. Kent Rgt. Bearers were sent up to both these places and arrangements made for the evacuation of the wounded.	

WAR DIARY
INTELLIGENCE SUMMARY

Army Form C. 2118.

Place	Date	Hour	Summary of Events and Information	Remarks and references to Appendices
	9/10/16		whole afternoon Captn BINNY, HOGG, LAUDER & KEROCH returned to the MEDICAL DUMP. At 3-30 p.m. I sent up a party of 50 Infantry to act as bearers and this evening a further party of 27 with 129 F.A. Casualties began to come in at 6 p.m. Stretcher cases have come in and I sitting only since 5:20 till 18 pm. & 6 pm. All stretcher cases were more of the 4th & 5th V-- 4 of these all stretcher cases were more of the 4th & 5th V-- numbers being today casualties 9 am 12 Noon yesterday to 12 Noon today. T officers and 246 O.R. Passed through. Capt. Corbill proceeded to relieve Lieut CONOLLY at THISTLE ALLEY at 9 A.M. The 139 F.A. bearers will be relieved at 5 p.m. today at the CORMIES POST. by the 13 F.2 F.A. bearers Under Lieut HUDSON till 9 A.M. today. Since 5 p.m. yesterday the following passed through stretcher cases and 6 5 casualties on the 9th & 6 up to 9 A.m. 10 aug 23 officers 412 + 5 OR 21 being 1750 PM from	15

Place	Date	Hour	Summary of Events and Information	Remarks and references to Appendices
	10/10/16		Relief. w/h 9B/19 F.A. of the 20th Division on taking over from one having Br. an advance party of the 9th F.A. will be at THISTLE ALLEY at 8 p.m. to be ready to take over when all our wounded have been evacuated. The bearer division will be at Mr. McCormics Post at 12 mid.n/t. The officer i/c McCormics Post will as soon as he is satisfied that all R.A. P.s have been properly relieved, and no more wounded of our Division remaining in front, ?? with the bearers to Med. D. Capt. Cowell on being relieved will return here. Relief to be completed at 4 A.m. on the 11th if possible. According to orders from A.D.M.S. N. 109 T. 10/10/16. I have detailed Lieut. D.A. DUFF R.A.M.C. to report with one orderly to the Corps School of Instruction ESCAR BONNEUSE for temporary duty. He will also at the a.a. p.m.n.n. for a copy and an A.B. of instructions & form according to him instructions.	[signature]

WAR DIARY or INTELLIGENCE SUMMARY

Army Form C. 2118.

Place	Date	Hour	Summary of Events and Information	Remarks and references to Appendices
	10/10/16		On the A.D.S. on S. H.I. Division. Since 5 p.m. yesterday 27 Stretcher cases passed through this A.D.S. who were on ground following gun return, wounded in the 4 & 8 Maltbay. An urgent wire was sent to me from POPPY stating that a considerable number of wounded were lying near FACTORY CORNER. An officer of the 23rd R.M.us. was sent as a guide to bearers from one CARMIES POST. A party was sent with the officer and the O i/c McCORMIES POST left without a bearer. Information was thus held up for the time being. I am afraid that there was only 6 cases [there]; half of the party of bearers was used to carry into Cases Down, the others were kept as reserve, this is only one instance of how I have been misinformed, as to casualties have been much exaggerated with the result that too many men were sent to one place, and the evacuation held up at times. Oct. By wire from KBS Lieut. D.G. DUFF has been detailed to proceed to CORPS. SCHOOL of Instruction at ESCAR BONNEUSE for temporary duty.	

WAR DIARY
or
INTELLIGENCE SUMMARY.
(Erase heading not required.)

Army Form C. 2118.

Place	Date	Hour	Summary of Events and Information	Remarks and references to Appendices
	10/16		Report of Operations on Oct. 7/12 1916. by order from No. A.D.M.S. 14th Division. On the night of Oct. 3/4. Oct. I relieved No 2 N.Z. Field Ambulance A.D.S, FLAT IRON COPSE, THISTLE ALLEY and McCORMIES Post. I had all my bearer posts early in the night and every thing working smoothly before 7 A.M. I called and detailed all officers and bearers of Oct. 135 & 140 T.A. (one two officers from each) 15 motor ambulance cars and 2 horse ambulance waggon. also 2 9 C.O. + 30 men from Sanitary Brigade attached to work with the ambulance bearers. Besides this I had 12 motor ambulance cars from No 2 M.A.C. and a number of char-a-bancs if required. I had also attached to men of the Sanitary Station and 4 N.C.O. from the Inf. Brigades to act as clerks in taking a nominal roll of all casualties of Oct. 41st Division.	True

Army Form C. 2118.

WAR DIARY
or
INTELLIGENCE SUMMARY.
(Erase heading not required.)

Place	Date	Hour	Summary of Events and Information	Remarks and references to Appendices
	10/10		The situation of the R.A.P.'s and M.O.'s were as follows Capt LOUDON 15 HANTS 122 Bde. & Lieut. WILLIAMSON 32 R.Fus. 124th Bde. on N&NE Road 300 yds left of TURK LANE. Lieut W. WILSON 12 EAST LANCS. 122 Bde. at M 20 b. 4.2. on TURK LANE. CAPT FULLER 10/12 QUEENS and Lieut HART 21st K.R.R.P. 124 Brigade at M 30 d. 7.4 yards off TURK LANE. CAPT HODSON 26/12 R.Fus. 124 Bde. near M 30 7.4. Capt ELIOT 15.KRR. 122 Bde. near where ABBEY Rd. crosses TURK LANE. Lieut LACY 11 R.W.K. 122nd Bde. at McCORMICKS POST. Lieut BROWN 120 R.F.A. Bde. at McCORMICKS POST. Disposition of Personnel of F.A°. 100 bearers of 115/12 F.A. with 32 Inf. bearers were in reserve at MEDICAL DUMP from 12 NOON on 9/10. 139th F.A. bearers with 140 R.A. bearers with 32 Inf. bearers attached to each were at THISTLE ALLEY at 5-30 A.M. on 10/10 instr. in charge of Capt. ROWBOTHOM. & Lieut TODD. ready to proceed to McCORMICKS POST.	ttot

WAR DIARY
or
INTELLIGENCE SUMMARY.

Place	Date	Hour	Summary of Events and Information	Remarks and references to Appendices
	10/7		At 6-30 a.m. Squad bearers were distributed as follows: to Capt. Rowbotham M.C. – 3 squads of bearers each to take R.A.P. beyond McCORMIC'S POST and 3 squads of 4 bearers each for each R.A.P. as above in rear of McCormic's Post. All the above worked between McCORMIC'S POST & R.A.P? only except when ordered to go forward to carry the remainder of the regimental stretcher bearers. The stretcher bearers S.Bs worked between McCORMIC'S POST and THISTLE ALLEY. The walking wounded carry was about 1¼ mls, and the carry from THISTLE ALLEY 1¾ mls. On no occasion did more than two regimental stretcher bearers form part of a squad. The Officer i/c of bearers was instructed to apply to the A.D.M.S. for more bearers through H.Q. of 124th Inf. Bde if required, and to report any casualties amongst personnel	Hwl

WAR DIARY
or
INTELLIGENCE SUMMARY.
(Erase heading not required.)

Army Form C. 2118.

Place	Date	Hour	Summary of Events and Information	Remarks and references to Appendices
	10/10/16		All leaves carried an overcoat, waterproof sheet and water bottle, and iron rations, also rations for 24 hrs. Capt. CORKILL was in command at THISTLE ALLEY assisted by Lieut THOMAS and the following officers detailed for duty at the Aid Dressing Corps — Capt. R.L. IMPEY, Lieut ROCH and Lieut DUFF. All regimental medical officers were supplied with a plentiful supply of surgical and medical material, drugs & medical comforts. A large supply of medical & surgical material, medical comforts, blankets & stretchers were constantly kept in readiness at Mc.CORMIC'S POST, THISTLE ALLEY and FLAT IRON COPSE as well as cookers, lamps, electric torches &c. Each officer & senior NCO was also supplied with one effective torch. As the wounded passed through A.D.S. Vy Mc.CORMIC'S POST, THISTLE ALLEY & FLAT IRON COPSE they received medical comforts as required.	hrs

WAR DIARY
or
INTELLIGENCE SUMMARY

Army Form C. 2118.

Place	Date	Hour	Summary of Events and Information	Remarks and references to Appendices
	10/10		Motor & evacuation employed from Thistle Alley to Corps Collecting Station for W.W. and Corps Main Dressing Station. Three horse ambulance wagons on always in readiness at Thistle Alley. As each horse ambulance wagon arrives at F.D.C. another was sent to Thistle Alley to allow there returning to rest. Motor ambulance cars were also in readiness to proceed to Thistle Alley if required. On arrival at Stan Corps the wounded were looked at by a M.O. while still in the wagon and if requiring no further treatment were transferred direct to the motor ambulance cars, and at the same time were given some hot tea, coffee, soup, bread, butter, sweet biscuits & cigarettes etc. These cars took them to either C.C.S for W.W. and Corps Main Dressing Station. A record was kept of all who passed through Thistle Alley & stan Corps.	Aug

23

Army Form C. 2118.

WAR DIARY
or
INTELLIGENCE SUMMARY.
(Erase heading not required.)

Place	Date	Hour	Summary of Events and Information	Remarks and references to Appendices
	10/6		There was chiefly a strafing action but served to alert numerous areas which otherwise would have escaped.	
			Actual Operations	
			The morning was very quiet till 1-45 p.m. when 2 or 4 hrs. commenced and gun teams very active. Wounded began to stream in at 5 p.m. and quickly increased in numbers. At 4-20 p.m. all our ambulances were on the road and about 20 w.w. waiting for evacuation so I wired for extra char-à-bancs according to orders from Q.M.S. 41 Div. At 9 p.m. a great number of wounded were pouring through and awaiting evacuation. I wired for 4 more chara-bancs and 6 motor ambulances which I found quite sufficient and soon was able to dispense with them.	
			During the afternoon Lieut. Macy at the 11th Royal Berks was wounded severely, and was helped into McCormick's Post and evacuated to M.D.S. there later on Capt. SHELDON of the	Ag. Ay

T 2134. Wt. W708-776. 500000. 4/15. Sir J. C. & S.

WAR DIARY
or
INTELLIGENCE SUMMARY.
(Erase heading not required.)

Army Form C. 2118.

Date	Hour	Summary of Events and Information	Remarks and references to Appendices
10/6		2/Lt R. Tux was sent sick by the C.O. for gastritis and general exhaustion; he was evacuated to C.R.S. The evacuation of wounded was continuous throughout the day. Saw on one lot reported melanee lilrium the genuine and the R.A.P. which appear to be due to want of sufficient regimental stretcher bearers to convey the wounded to the R.A.P. Personally inspected these aid posts myself and found the men alert in full swing. M 30 & 7.2 had only one wounded man for evacuation at 2 p.m. M 30d. 7.4. had two resting in a dug-out till the morning being light cases. The evacuation at gun-time was slow due to all the bearers being dog tired. As far as I could gather there were about 30 or 30 wounded still in the front line which were eventually evacuated on the 5th, 9th & 10th inst.	Appx

Army Form C. 2118.

WAR DIARY
or
INTELLIGENCE SUMMARY.
(Erase heading not required.)

Place	Date	Hour	Summary of Events and Information	Remarks and references to Appendices
	10/9/16		During this attack the Officers, bearers and stretcher divisions worked in a manner worthy of all praise. Many of the squads carried for nearly 2 miles in four different trips which meant carrying about 11 miles with wounded on stretchers and this was our own ground so uneven and slippery that only those who have tried carrying a stretcher on it can appreciate its great difficulties of it all. On 6 A.m. on Sept 5th Sept 13th ½ A bearers arrived to relieve us. 139½ + 140 ½ units to A.D.S. field who proceeded to MEDICAL — DUMP for rest. Lieut Roach relieved Capt Rowbotham + Lieut Hood at the Cormies Post. Lieut Duff relieved Capt Cowell at Trialts Alley. During the day parties of Infantry under Capt Laudry Hogg were sent up to clear the front line of wounded an infinite care in after a considerable number of wounded were lying out. I sent Capt Jordan forward to enquire into this and found that there were only 6 cases waiting for	Hay

WAR DIARY
or
INTELLIGENCE SUMMARY.
(Erase heading not required.)

Army Form C. 2118.

Place	Date	Hour	Summary of Events and Information	Remarks and references to Appendices
	10/16		organisation and this was at once dealt with. During the following day (9+10/15) other cases were found in the front line bringing the number up to about 27 who were wounded on the 7th & 8th. The following is the total number of wounded that have passed through the A.D.S. at Fir Tree from cases. Oct 4th — Oct 5th — Oct 6th — Oct 7th — Oct 8th — Oct 9th — Oct 10th — 106. 5.94 253 Total 1164. 194. The following officers I submitted to you as on I.O.1st recommendation as follows:— Capt. R.F. Jarry R.A.M.C. for D.S.O for good work at the SHRINE, FLEURS, & the organisation of the bearers on and about TURK LANE. Frequently under shell fire. Capt J.L. Cahill R.A.M.C. S.R. for Military X for good work at the SHRINE & FLEURS frequently under shell fire the Run. E. Thomas C.F. for good work at SHRINE + THISTLE ALLEY. for midwinter X.	Hay

Army Form C. 2118.

WAR DIARY
or
INTELLIGENCE SUMMARY.
(Erase heading not required.)

Instructions regarding War Diaries and Intelligence Summaries are contained in F.S. Regs., Part II. and the Staff Manual respectively. Title pages will be prepared in manuscript.

Place	Date	Hour	Summary of Events and Information	Remarks and references to Appendices
	10/9		and the following NCOs + men who were hammer heavy shell fire Sergt Palmer for Military medal, for excellent work also leading his men on the right of FLEURS on the 25th & 26th Septr and 100 yds and again on the left of FLEURS on the 10th Oct also Pte Green + Pte Bradley on the same occasions — for excellent work and volunteering on several occasions them men was added for doing the following duties — Pte Phillips Sergt Golding Sgt Peacock for Pte Morris Pte Mathews Pte Webb Pte High Pte Poole Pte Alma Pte Carlson O. Pte Stephenett Pte Rutland Pte Crayton Pte Oakhurst Pte Munro Pte Sanborn Fr. Pte Stephens J. Pte Wilson Pte Bradley Pte Saunders R. Pte Spence Pte Hill H.W. Pte Seaman Pte Harlock Pte Brown	Sgt

WAR DIARY
INTELLIGENCE SUMMARY

Army Form C. 2118.

Place	Date	Hour	Summary of Events and Information	Remarks and references to Appendices
	11/10		Paraded with transport during the morning at 8.30. at 10.15 am carried cook-ing and ration position of all the R.A.M.C. to which stretcher bearers were tied at the time relief was completed and all wounded evacuated. As A.D.M.S. 3 Div. gave operation order No 6. the 123rd C.C.S. in [illegible] at that same wagon instead of at POMMIERS CAMP. I find there is no room in that camp so return to Brigade to MEDICAL DUMP. I have repeated any position to Brigade Major. 12.15 Lt. 13er. Green but am aware if I may remain here. Reply from A.D.M.S. – Yes.	
			As per corps order No 6. Capt H. CORKILL with Bearers [illegible] proceeded to C.R.S. for duty. I append to OO 27½ M.A.C. for horse as they are utterly done up but have been refused. I also applied to the A.D.M.S. acting for Chun to not till the morning of the 12th without success.	
	12/10		As per O.O. No 6. I have detailed Lieut G.T. Roma and what remains of R. Tent Sub-Divn to proceed to Area E.14.b.	[illegible]

WAR DIARY
or
INTELLIGENCE SUMMARY.
(Erase heading not required.)

Army Form C. 2118.

Place	Date	Hour	Summary of Events and Information	Remarks and references to Appendices
	12/10/16		continued. Capt. CHISNEY & Capt. W.M. BIDEN have been noted to G. any still turbulence. The Corps Commander whilst appreciating the acts of gallantry performed by Capt. W.M. Carvill considers that such gallantry does not quite reach the standard required to merit immediate reward. It desired however their names may be forwarded for inclusion in a general despatch when cases of par. to A/G 1049 7/10/16. issued.	
	13/10/16		Arrived with the 123rd Inf. Bde at DERNANCOURT and encamped closely. Capt. A. ASHMORE has joined my unit. Capt. W.M. BIDEN is detailed by the A.D.M.S. to relieve Capt. Elliott in on/a of 18th K.R.R. as per A.D.M.S. No 40/18/m dt. 13/10/16.	
	14/10/16		New reinforcements have arrived bringing up strength up to above normal. Day spent in rest.	40½

WAR DIARY or INTELLIGENCE SUMMARY

Army Form C. 2118.

Place	Date	Hour	Summary of Events and Information	Remarks and references to Appendices
DERNANCOURT	15/10/16		Lieut D.G. Tuft R.A.M.C. returned from the Corps School of Instruction. Capt. Chinnery proceeded to WAREL as billeting officer.	
"	16/10/16		Parade service 9-30 A.M. Transport as per 123rd Bde Order No 19 dated 15/10/16 moved off by 8-30 A.M. and arrived at ST SAUVEUR at 6-30 p.m. The remainder of the F.A. moved to Rest Camp north of DERNANCOURT for the night. 13 cases sub-division returned from the C.R.S.	
"	17/10/16		Transport departed from ST SAUVEUR at 12 Noon. and arrived at WANEL at 9-30 p.m. The remainder of F.A. less motor ambulance cars entrained at EDGEHILL at 5 p.m. according to 41st Div. No 252/S.7. 14/10/16. Capt J.A. Carville proceeded to HAZEBROUCK as billeting officer arriving there at 11 p.m. on the 15th and proceeded to GODWAERSVELDE to meet units.	
"	18/10/16		Arrived at OISEMONT at 12-30 p.m. after an exceedingly slow journey entrained there and arrived at WANEL at 5 p.m.	
WANEL	19/10/16		Rest at WANEL.	

WAR DIARY
or
INTELLIGENCE SUMMARY.
(Erase heading not required.)

Army Form C. 2118.

Place	Date	Hour	Summary of Events and Information	Remarks and references to Appendices
	19/10/16		H.A. departed entrained from WANEL at 5 pm (Transport) and at 9-30 pm (personnel) for PONT REMY Ry. Sta.	
	20/10/16		Entrained at 2-15 A.M. having taken 2½ hours to load Motor Lorries with our horses & wagons, by means of ramps. Arrived at GODWAERSVELDE at 10-15 A.M. and moved into billets at HUGEDEORN Sheet. 27 Q.23.a.4.4. and reported arrival to A.D.M.S. at FLETRE. Paid a visit to & attended a conference at FLETRE. All N.C.O.'d men allowed out up to 5 p.m.	
	21/10/16		Been over in the 2d Army Area, having passed from the XV Corps, 4th ARMY, through 10th CORPS. By order from A.D.M.S. CAPT CHESNEY has been detailed as D.A.D.M.S. during the absence on leave of Major Thruston, from the 15th inst. On the 20th the M.T. (proceeded) to HUGEDEORN FARM. Via VIGNACOURT–DOULLENS–ST POL–ANVIN–ST HILAIRE–AIRE–HAZEBROUCK–+ FLETRE.	Not ≡

WAR DIARY or INTELLIGENCE SUMMARY

Army Form C. 2118.

Place	Date	Hour	Summary of Events and Information	Remarks and references to Appendices
	22/10/16		41st 2 Division's G. 12 Noon 30 & September 1916.	
			Officers. Other Ranks	
			Killed Wounded missing Killed Wounded missing Evacuated Sick	
			5 13 – 2 428 2362 810 235.	
			The 15th K.R.R. suffered most. Any ambulance had 9 wounded and 6 evacuated sick.	
			Capt. H. Corkill has been detailed to proceed to OXELAERE for instruction in Anti-gas measures.	
	22/10/16		R.A.M.C. Operation Order No. 7. dt. 22/10/16. Para. 3. B. 139th F.A. will relieve the 12th Australian F.A. M.A. the O.C. arranging time + date.	
			(a) in the evacuation from the BRASSERIE RAPP. (N6.a.1.)	
			(b) and take over the VIERSTRAAT A.D.S. (N4.d.00)	
			(c) and main dressing station at LA CLYTE (N9 c 4.3)	
			(d) and relieve the walking & sitters at RIDGEWOOD (N5 a 5.5) and BRASSERIE (N6 a 2.2)	

Place	Date	Hour	Summary of Events and Information	Remarks and references to Appendices
	22/10/16		Operation order No 7 attached.	
			139 ½ F.A. Operation Order No 1.	
			Section A under Capt R.E. Jomfrey will parade at 9 A.M. on the 23rd and be ready to move off at 9-30 A.M.	
			The Motor Ambulances and one Dispatch rider will accompany this section.	
			On arrival at LA CLYTE Lt Bearer Sub-division under Lieut at Thomas, assisted by Lieut A.G. Duff will proceed to A.D.S. at VIERSTRAAT	
			Lieut A.P. Thomas will detail 1 NCO and 12 men to proceed RAP's at the BRASSERIE.	
			He will also detail one Pte on Water Warden at the BRASSERIE N 6.a.2.2. and one at RIDGE WOOD N 5 a 5.5.	
			A Tent sub-division will remain at LA CLYTE One limber of A sect. will remain behind, the remainder of the tt will move off at 5 A.M on the morning of the 24 and proceed to LA CLYTE.	Haig

WAR DIARY or INTELLIGENCE SUMMARY

Army Form C. 2118.

Place	Date	Hour	Summary of Events and Information	Remarks and references to Appendices
	10/22/16		MEDICAL ARRANGEMENTS 41st Division attached. 13 cases were evacuated by M.A.C. to No 6 London F.A. This evening including Sergt. Major Baugham & Mathews. A section proceeded to Bray in detailed in Divisional Order No 1.	
	10/23/16		At 22°C by 6 p.m. Capt. Donkey had completely taken over and every-thing was in good working order — The 1/2 Aus. F.A. having departed from huby left HUGEDEORN FARM at 5-40 p.m. and arrived at La Clytte at 10 A.M. One despatch rider sent to A.D.M.S. with his motor cycle for duty there. Sergeant PALMER R.a. proceeded on 10 days leave. Lieut D.G. Duff R.a. relieved Lieut R.A. Fuller RAMC No. 1/2 10/2 Queens 124th Bde.	
	10/24/16		Capt. A. ASHMORE R.a. relieved Lieut C.G. Duff at the A.D.S. Capt. Donkey proceeded to the A.D.S. & R.A.P. to see if they were working properly. [struck through] Transferred to J.R.S. 41st Division Sgt. 13 cases at No 6 London F.A. Some Sergt Major Baugham A.S.C. & Mathews R.a.m.c. to all to be moved	that

WAR DIARY
or
INTELLIGENCE SUMMARY.
(Erase heading not required.)

Army Form C. 2118.

Instructions regarding War Diaries and Intelligence Summaries are contained in F. S. Regs., Part II. and the Staff Manual respectively. Title pages will be prepared in manuscript.

Place	Date	Hour	Summary of Events and Information	Remarks and references to Appendices
	25/10		All spare men engaged in drawing bricks for the Ravelines, creating a shed for the R.A.E. equipments, and other minor improvements. Capt. FULLER M.O. 10th Queens proceeded on leave to-day (Contrexeau).	
	26/10		Lieut. R.T. Todd has been detailed to proceed to STEENVOORDE with B. Section to take over (1) a Divisional Hospital in Rue de CARNOT, and organize it for treatment of sick & serious sufferers & details passing through. (2) Baths in the same street and review the Town major in the running of steam - (3) a water point at P 12. a 5.4. which is looked after by 2 R.A.M.C. men who act as water bearers. Capt. Connolly and party of the 138th F.A. will on relief rejoin the Q.R. & at WIPPENHOEK. proceed to STEENVOORDE and make a thorough inspection of the Hospital, Baths, and water point, and obtained a	too

Place	Date	Hour	Summary of Events and Information	Remarks and references to Appendices
	26/6		continued a farm field & huttments for the A.R.C. & Transport close behind the church. The house for a D.R. is an excellent one and can be made very comfortable if the heating apparatus & radiators can be put in order. All cases requiring evacuation will be sent to the C.C.S. at PONT REMY, except those of the 41st Div'n unless they specially require evacuation. Present the insufficient accommodation of the Baths is the way of a dressing room, changing room & ironing room but has been got at & that nothing can be done as there Baths are only on loan as a matter of favour.	
	27/6		Capt. V.K. Cartell proceeded to STEEN VOORDE to take over the detention hospital and Baths as — by order from 4th A.D.M.S. Lieut Tedd will remain to assist till further orders.	

34

Army Form C. 2118.

WAR DIARY
or
INTELLIGENCE SUMMARY.
(Erase heading not required.)

Place	Date	Hour	Summary of Events and Information	Remarks and references to Appendices
	27/10		Squeezed in the morning to make a reconnaissance of area through which our wounded are evacuated from the trenches to M.D.S. at LA CLYTTE — a copy of report forwarded sent to A.D.M.S. as requested.	
	28/10		Visited by Col. Sutton D.D.M.S. Xth Corps. This morning. Inspected all our accommodation both for sick and wounded, with the A.D.M.S., and noted specially that there is no accommodation for officers when sick, or wounded — also no stoves on the ambulance huts.	
	29/10		Capt. W.M. @ HESNEY returned from the A.D.M.S. today. Capt. S.S.q. Wight reported himself for duty by order from the A.D.M.S. Capt. W.M. Biden R.A.M.C has been posted permanently to 31 W.N.R.R.C. I have arranged with the C.R.E. 2. OUDERDOM. for an officer to superintend the construction of the new latrines.	yes

T.2134. Wt. W708–776. 500000. 4/15. Sir J. C. & S.

WAR DIARY or INTELLIGENCE SUMMARY

Army Form C. 2118.

Place	Date	Hour	Summary of Events and Information	Remarks and references to Appendices
	29/10/16		I sent in to GHQ 2nd Echn. a list of OR personnel my 4.A. dislikes & recommends for higher rates of corps pay.	
	30/10/16		Capt. R.S. Janney and I visited YPRES this morning. Today's sent in a list of NCOs and men recommended for promotion. It's completed. OC war establishment. A live burst at about 10-30 P.M. in the R.E. G/9m. single officer's quarters of OC R.A.M.C. Lieutenants. On account of this find leaving WC several shred rapidly to an adjoining hut and given to a stretcher moved home of the village and completely gutted it.	
	31/10/16		Capt. R.S. Janney R.a. proceeded on 10 days leave to England. Since taking over 71 sick + 6 wounded have passed through this M.D.S. an average of 2 wounded per day.	

Wisdom Lt Col. R.a.m.c.
O.C. 139 (2) Field Ambulance.

140/1943.

4th Div.

CONFIDENTIAL Vol 7

War Diary

of

139th Field Ambulance

Volume VII

November 1916.

Nov. 1916.

COMMITTEE FOR THE
MEDICAL HISTORY OF THE WAR
Date 13 MAR. 1917

WAR DIARY or INTELLIGENCE SUMMARY

Army Form C. 2118.

VOL VIII
Nov. 1916.

Place	Date	Hour	Summary of Events and Information	Remarks and references to Appendices
	1/11/16		The following changes have taken place to-day. Capt. E.J. ELLIOTT R.A.M.C. has taken over charge of A.D.S. from Lieut. BRYDEN R.A.M.C. who returned sick for duty. Capt. W.M. CHESNEY has relieved Capt. H.M. BIDEN R.A.M.C. M.O. to 18th K.R.R.C. and Capt. H.M. BIDEN has reported here for duty. Capt. A. ASHMORE R.A.M.C. has reported to A.D.M.S. 23rd Division for duty. Lieut. R.T. TODD is now in charge of Detention Hospital and Baths.	
STEENVOORDE	2/11/16		Most of my men employed on horse lines, and A.D.S. Some have gone to YPRES for bricks.	
	3/11/16		35 M.O.O. and men have returned from attention hospital STEENVORDE. 2/Lieut. D. WALKER 12 EAST SURREY evacuated to No 4 C.C.S. for suspected Rose measles. Precautionary measures taken to prevent spread of infection. Visited by A.D.C., D.D.M.S. and A.D.M.S.	

Army Form C. 2118.

WAR DIARY
or
INTELLIGENCE SUMMARY.
(Erase heading not required.)

Place	Date	Hour	Summary of Events and Information	Remarks and references to Appendices
	4/16		The unit has been reallotted as far as possible. Arrangements have been made with R.E. 225th Coy. for:-	
			1. Completion of horse-standings & run for Antis.	
			2. The erecting of a wagon standing along side the	
			3. The erection of a drying shed alongside the large hut near corner of road.	
			4. The erection of two wood houses (one for personnel & one for patients) (a) one for personnel to be between butcher shop and the large hut.	
			(b) one for patients to be in courtyard behind school	
			5. Cook house for patients in present hut close to geen store by raising the roof.	
			6. Repair of present A.D.S.	
			7. Repair of present kitchen	
			8. Conversion of kitchen near the road into a butcher shop.	

WAR DIARY
or
INTELLIGENCE SUMMARY.

Army Form C. 2118.

Place	Date	Hour	Summary of Events and Information	Remarks and references to Appendices
	5/6		Lieut R.T. TODD R.A.M.C. returned to M.O.'s having been relieved by Lieut. C.A.P.T. Rowe.	
			Disposition of 124 Inf Bde + 139 L A.	
		10.03am	Queen's R.W.S. Right sub sector of line	
			21 Bn K.R.R.C. " " " " "	
		26/12 R.E. Inc " " " " "	
		3.2. do. two		
		20/12 D.L.I. mis uffeant at RIDGEWOOD,		
			in Reserve at LA CLYTTE	
			On the Right of 2193m N.R.R.C.	
			Bn. 124 M.G. Coy + 124 L.T.M. Bty. on fixed spot.	
			R.A.M.C.	
			1 NCO + L/S squads of four men each at the BRASSERIES.	
			At A.D.S.	
			Capt Elliott	
			Shane O.C. 1 Sergt, 2 Cooks, 2 Stores 2 Bearers 2 Sanitary men and 2 Water Carriers. Also 10 men in reserve —	
			Detention Hospital STEENVOORDE one M.O. and 2NCO + 13 R.A.M.C	
			1 NCO + 6 A.S.C. H.T.	
			1 M.T.A.S.C. Driver	

Army Form C. 2118.

WAR DIARY
or
INTELLIGENCE SUMMARY.
(Erase heading not required.)

Place	Date	Hour	Summary of Events and Information	Remarks and references to Appendices
	5/16		MAIN DRESSING STATION, LA CLYTTE. O.C. Capt. T.M. CORKILL Capt. H.M. BIDEN 2nd Lt. R.T. TODD and (Capt RL IMPEY on leave), and the remainder of the M.A. Have sent three men (two K.R.R. and one R.F.A) to replace my Walon Wardens at STEENVOORDE RIDGEWOOD & BRASSERIES.	
	6/16		LIEUT. C.M. SCOTT R.A.M.C. Recommended sick to A.R.S. WIPPENHOEK on the 5/16 CAPT. T.W. SHELDON R.A.M.C. Arrived from contract leave and has been granted four temporary duty to the 20th D.F.T. Found in the well in the base yard by the Mess Servants about a hundred litres of Queronne of the 12 June, T.A. I have reported it to the O.C.	
	11/16		LIEUT. D.P. THOMAS R.A.M.C. a part of attention Hospital STEENVOORDE has been relieved by the 69 M.A.C. 232 Division. He has a forty armed lorry for duty. I visited the A.D.S. and one R.A.P. a Telephone is now installed connecting the R.A.P. BRASSERIES	

WAR DIARY
or
INTELLIGENCE SUMMARY.
(Erase heading not required.)

Army Form C. 2118.

Place	Date	Hour	Summary of Events and Information	Remarks and references to Appendices
	7/16		and A.D.S. to M.D.S. La Clytte. Also to H.Q. 41 Division and H.Q. of each R.B. Have taken over the duties as A.D.M.S. from Col.	
	8/16		Major RATTRAY R.A.M.C. on leave — was over on the stables and other works still in progress. Capt. W.M. BIDEN has relieved Capt. S.E.Y. ELLIOTT of the A.D.S. Capt. ELLIOTT has returned here for duty.	
	9/16		Lieut. D.G. DUF R.A.M.C. has been relieved by the return of Capt. R.E. FOLEY, and has returned to the Ambulance New constructions were deleme for the bettering of the existing medical accommodation and evacuation in the area occupied by this Division. So evening parties as to be provided from the 7A. so fellows 50 from D.R.S. (135 FA) 25 each from 135 & 140 F.A. in addition to the parts already W. A.D.S. VIERSTRAAT. KILLED WOUNDED MISSING + EVACUATED SICK during Oct. 1916. see over page.	

WAR DIARY or INTELLIGENCE SUMMARY

Army Form C. 2118.

Place	Date	Hour	Summary of Events and Information	Remarks and references to Appendices
	9/7/16		Officers Other ranks	
			Killed wounded missing Killed Wounded Missing Executed P.O.W.	Total
			26 75 7 405 1613 253 351	1261
			Out of the above the following are the R.A.M.C. casualties	
	7A 138		— — — 9 — —	4
	7A 135		— — — — 9 —	8
	7A 140		1 — — 11 — —	7
			Of the above 9 = 114 Q.W.R. Regt. supplied advance supply	
	R.7 &		— — 6.2 242 55	9
			Under authority granted by His Majesty the King the Corps Commander has awarded the military Medal to the under mentioned who have been announced on Parade to-day.	
			69314 Q2 F. BRADLEY 135½ Field Ambulance	
			74523 Pte S.S. MOORE " " "	
			6544 Q2 W.H. PALMER " " "	
			The A.D.M.S. offers his congratulations to these & the Corps & Divisional Commanders.	

WAR DIARY
or
INTELLIGENCE SUMMARY.
(Erase heading not required.)

Army Form C. 2118.

Place	Date	Hour	Summary of Events and Information	Remarks and references to Appendices
	10/11/16		Disposition of Officers & Men 18th & 19th Jan'y & the 125th Sect during of 127th Fd Amb and Regtl Stretcher Bearers:	
			1. 32nd Bn Royal Sus. Right Sub-section	
			M.O. Lieut Williamson at R.A.P. VIERSTRAAT.	
			Distribution of Regtl Stretcher Bearers: 2 in trench line & support line & Reserve line 4. Regt & R.A.P. 2.	
			2. 26th Bn Royal Sus. Left Sub-section	
			M.O. Lieut Foley at R.A.P. BRASSERIES.	
			Distribution of rifle Stretcher bearers & trench line & support line & Reserve line at Hd.Qrs. & R.A.P. 2.	
			3. 12th Bn Yorks & Lancs Right. In supt of 26th Royal Sus.	
			M.O. Lieut ____ at 10mm	
			Distribution of rifle Stretch bearers, trench line & support line & Reserve line to Hd Qrs & R.A.P. 2.	
			4. 21 Bn Kings Royal Rifle Corps. In support RIDGE WOOD.	
			M.O. Lieut Hall at R.A.P. RIDGE WOOD.	

Place	Date	Hour	Summary of Events and Information	Remarks and references to Appendices
	10/16		5. 10th Rl. Queen. R.W. Surrey Regt. in reserve at LACLYTTE. M.O. Lieut R.E. FULLER. Evacuation from the Bressaires. One NCO with 1st squad & 4 men each of R.A.M.C conduct the sick & wounded to the A.D.S by trolly or by walking. Squads changed weekly. Advanced Dressing Station. M.O. Capt J.S. M'Rider R.a.m.c. and Capt. T.H. EWELL 1 NCO, 2 bearer 2 cooks & dresser 2 sanitary 1 wash 1 ambulance driver with orderly and 6 men in reserve (changed weekly sent the sick). Fatigue party of 1 NCO + 20 men changed weekly. Main Dressing Station. He. 129/D ft. Capt. S.E.Y. ELLIOTT, Capt. R.L. IMPEY, Lieut R.T. TODD, Lieut D.G.THOMAS, Lieut O.G. DUFF. 10 NCO + 42 men fatigue parties 1 NCO & 65 men	

WAR DIARY
or
INTELLIGENCE SUMMARY.
(Erase heading not required.)

Army Form C. 2118.

Place	Date	Hour	Summary of Events and Information	Remarks and references to Appendices
	11/7/16		Capt R.T. Jenkyn R.A.M.C. Ron returned from leave. Lieut Col. Hurlong Same + Lieut R.T. Todd have departed for 10 days leave and 14 days respectively.	
	12/7/16		Lieut. D.C. DUFF + a party of 9. 20 O.R's attended 123 Inf Brigade Parade for the presentation of medal ribbons at 9.30 AM. Sgt W.H PALMER + L/Cpl S.S.MOORE were presented with Military Medal ribbons. L/Cpl F BRADLEY who is at present on leave will be presented with a M.M ribbon at a later date	
			Capt T.F. CORKILL went to A.D.S VIERSTRAAT for duty	
			M.O.S. + A.D.S were visited by Corps General + D.D.M.S.	R.L.J

Army Form C. 2118.

WAR DIARY
or
INTELLIGENCE SUMMARY.
(Erase heading not required.)

Instructions regarding War Diaries and Intelligence Summaries are contained in F.S. Regs., Part II. and the Staff Manual respectively. Title pages will be prepared in manuscript.

Place	Date	Hour	Summary of Events and Information	Remarks and references to Appendices
	12/7/16		A relief party from 73 Section has been sent up to the A.D.S.	
	13/7/16		The Stables were inspected by the Army Commandant, who gave permission for the horses to be put in at once. The engineering party who were working for us are done. The engineering party for the present owing to lack of material has been withdrawn.	
	15/7/16		10th Bn "Queens" R.W.S. Regt relieved 32nd Bn Royal Fusiliers on the right & the 21st Bn K.R.R.C. relieved the 25th Bn Royal Fusiliers on the left of the Right Sector	
	16/7/16		Capt W.M. BIDEN relieved to M.D.S. being relieved at A.D.S. by Lieut D.G. DUFF	

WAR DIARY
or
INTELLIGENCE SUMMARY.
(Erase heading not required.)

Army Form C. 2118.

Place	Date	Hour	Summary of Events and Information	Remarks and references to Appendices
	18/7/16		Lieut D.G. DUFF appointed to O.C. 183 Bgy R.F.A. for present duty as M.O. Capt. S.E.Y. ELLIOTT sent to A.D.S. in place of Lieut DUFF	
	19/7/16		Lieut D.P. THOMAS took over permanent medical charge of 189th Bgy R.F.A. M.D.S. was visited by A.D.M.S. & Staff Officer	
	20/7/16		Capt. 7.J. CORKILL & R.L. IMREY made front line trenches & chm position for 2 horse relay dumps, one at POPPY DUMP & the other at BOIS CARRE communication Tunnel.	

WAR DIARY or INTELLIGENCE SUMMARY.

Army Form C. 2118.

Place	Date	Hour	Summary of Events and Information	Remarks and references to Appendices
	21/11		The 32 Bn Royal Fusiliers relieves 10th Bn Queens on the right & the 26th Bn Royal Fusiliers relieves 21st Bn K.R.R.S on the left of Right sub.	
			Copy of Operation Orders for night of 22nd November	
			1. Object	
			Two R.A.M.C. bearer dumps will be established, one at POPPY DUMP and another at BOIS CARRE Communication Tunnel in order to	
			(a) hasten the evacuation of wounded	
			(b) lighten the work of the Regimental bearers	
			II Strength	
			(a) Lt. PALMER with 16 O.R.s will be at POPPY DUMP	
			(b) Lt. SHANNON with 12 O.R.s at BOIS CARRE Communication Tunnel	R.S.

III Equipment.
(a) H Stretchers will be taken to each dump
(b) Greatcoats & blankets were expended to be worn
(c) Each man will carry a sling.
(d) Water bottle haversack on S.B. carriers

IV PARTY DUMP PARTY
(a) Two parts will be in position ½ hour before Zero hour
(b) Walking wounded will be directed to R.D.S
(c) Stretcher cases will be taken over from Regimental bearers — a stretcher being given in return — & taken to the R.D.S.
(d) The Stretcher squads will be numbered & a second man placed in charge of each
(e) As each squad leaves with a stretcher case the NCO in charge will note its number & time of departure
(f) The time of the return of each squad will also be noted
(g) These figures will be handed in to the CO on the following day

2/7/16

Army Form C. 2118.

WAR DIARY
or
INTELLIGENCE SUMMARY.
(Erase heading not required.)

Place	Date	Hour	Summary of Events and Information	Remarks and references to Appendices
	21/1/16		**V BOIS CARRE & T. Party**	
			(a) This party will be in position ½ hour before zero hour	
			(b) Walking wounded will be directed to A.D.S.	
			(c) Stretcher cases will be taken down on trolley, two men going to each trolley	
			(d) These men will take the trolley as far as the BRASSERIE from where two men R.A.M.C. from the BRASSERIE will take the trolley on to the A.D.S.	
			(e) In both cases the NCO i/c will note the times of departure & return of men taking cases down	
			(f) Should there be no trollies available stretcher cases will be carried to the R.A.P. at BRASSERIE & thence to A.D.S	
			VI Transport Two motor ambulance cars will be stationed at A.D.S. from 8.0 PM to 6.0AM	

WAR DIARY
or
INTELLIGENCE SUMMARY.
(Erase heading not required.)

Army Form C. 2118.

Place	Date	Hour	Summary of Events and Information	Remarks and references to Appendices
			VII Treatment (1) A.T.S will only be given at M.D.S. (2) Hot tea, bovril etc will be kept in readiness for patients for one hour after Zero hour onwards.	
			VIII Zero hour. Zero hour will be notified later as "Zero hour means Bologne at ... pm"	
			IX 2/c NCO's i/c Dumps will not leave until they have ascertained that there are no more wounded up the line.	
			R.A. Smyth?	
			O.C 139th Field Amb 5.30 PM 21.11.16	

WAR DIARY
or
INTELLIGENCE SUMMARY
(Erase heading not required.)

Army Form C. 2118

Place	Date	Hour	Summary of Events and Information	Remarks and references to Appendices
	22/10		Visits by A.D.M.S. & D.A.D.M.S. who inspected the men & horses during stables	
			In the afternoon a conference of the M.O.s of the Division was held at the Headquarters of 140th Field Ambulance. Capts. T J Conkill & R L Impey attended from 139th Field Amb.	
	24/10		Second conference held by A.D.M.S., Capts W M Biden & S E Y Elliott attended	
	25/10		12nd Inf Bty Route postponed until further notice	
	26/10		Lieut R T Todd returned from his contract leave	
	27/10		A party of 1 NCO & 15 O.R.s, from 139th F.D., started work on a new R.A.P. at VIERSTRAAT	

Army Form C. 2118

WAR DIARY
or
INTELLIGENCE SUMMARY

(Erase heading not required.)

Instructions regarding War Diaries and Intelligence Summaries are contained in F. S. Regs., Part II. and the Staff Manual respectively. Title Pages will be prepared in manuscript.

Place	Date	Hour	Summary of Events and Information	Remarks and references to Appendices
	27/11		Capt. T.J. CORKILL return to M.D.S. for duty. Being relieved at the A.D.S. by Lieut. R.T. TODD.	
	28/11		Extract from R.A.M.C. Routine Orders dated 26th Nov. 1916 (No 219) "Major (Temp Lieut Colonel) H.W. Long R.A.M.C, late Officer Commanding 139th Field Ambulance, relinquishes the temporary rank of Lieut Colonel 7 weeks to the substantive rank of major from 21st inst, on ceasing to hold the appointment of O.C. a Field Ambulance — 5 reason of being pronted sick leave in England in extension of ordinary sick leave — " Appointment (No 220) "Capt R.L. IMPEY R.A.M.C (R) is appointed in acting command of the 139th Field Ambulance, pending a permanent appointment. Command to date from 22nd November 1916."	RL2

1875 Wt. W593/826 1,000,000 4/15 J.B.C. & A. A.D.S.S./Forms/C. 2118.

WAR DIARY
or
INTELLIGENCE SUMMARY

(Erase heading not required.)

Army Form C. 2118

Place	Date	Hour	Summary of Events and Information	Remarks and references to Appendices
	29/11/16		Capt W. M. BIDEN went to A.D.S. for duty. Lieut R.T. TODD returned to M.D.S.	
	30/11/16		Temp Lieut R.T. TODD promoted to Temp Captain. 2nd London Fd Amb Capt R.T. TODD. went as Company M.O. to 15th HANTS Reg relieving Lieut HUDSON returning on 10 days leave. Attached operations orders for night of December 2nd	A19

R.L. Scott
Capt 139th Field Amb

19/1943.

41st Div.

Dec. 19th

Confidential

Vol 8

War Diary
of
139th Field Ambulance

COMMITTEE FOR THE
MEDICAL HISTORY OF THE WAR
Date 13 MAR. 1917

3 Dec - 31516

From Dec. 1st /16

VOLUME viii

Army Form C. 2118.

WAR DIARY
or
INTELLIGENCE SUMMARY.
(Erase heading not required.)

VOL IX

Place	Date	Hour	Summary of Events and Information	Remarks and references to Appendices
	1/12/16		Capt S.E.Y. ELLIOTT went to 18th K.R.R.s as temporary M.O. in place of Capt CHESNEY who is sick.	
			Conference of C.O.s held by A.D.M.S.	
			Distribution of 139th Field Amb.	
			Main Party at LA CLYTTE — 3 Officers 98 men	
			Working " " VIERSTRAAT (ADS) — 28	
			" " (RAP) — 17	
			" " (ADS) 1 16	
			B Section at BRASSERIE (RAP) — 9	
			" " RIDGEWOOD 1	
			" " BRASSERIE 1	
			Leave — 5	
			Cyclist Orderly 1	
			Detention 1	
			4 177	

Army Form C. 2118

WAR DIARY
or
INTELLIGENCE SUMMARY
(Erase heading not required.)

Instructions regarding War Diaries and Intelligence Summaries are contained in F. S. Regs., Part II. and the Staff Manual respectively. Title Pages will be prepared in manuscript.

Place	Date	Hour	Summary of Events and Information	Remarks and references to Appendices
	1/3/16		2nd Bry Battalions disposed as follows —	
			124th Bry R Quarters — Right Subsector	
			3.2nd Bn R Quarters — " "	
			2.6th " R " — Left "	
			2.1st Bn KRR — In support RIDGEWOOD	
			10th " Queens — In reserve LA CLYTTE	

Army Form C. 2118

WAR DIARY
or
INTELLIGENCE SUMMARY
(Erase heading not required.)

Instructions regarding War Diaries and Intelligence Summaries are contained in F.S. Regs., Part II. and the Staff Manual respectively. Title Pages will be prepared in manuscript.

Place	Date	Hour	Summary of Events and Information	Remarks and references to Appendices
	2/12/16		Capt T.R TODD returned to the unit reporting sick	
	3/12/16		On the night of the 2nd the Rue 7 the 32nd RJ's came off. Two parties of Ambulance bearers were sent up to help the Regimental bearers. One party of 18 men were stationed at POPPY DUMP hay on horse before Gun Line — 12.35 A.M. A second party of 14 were posted at BOIS CARRÉ communication tunnel. The first wounded reached POPPY DUMP about 1.15 A.M. The walking cases were directed to the A.D.S. when the wounds were dressed & if hot drink given to each man. The first batch of walking wounded arrived at M.D.S. at 2.45 A.M.	

Army Form C. 2118

WAR DIARY
or
INTELLIGENCE SUMMARY

(Erase heading not required.)

Place	Date	Hour	Summary of Events and Information	Remarks and references to Appendices
	2/12/16		Capentes & Choristes. There were at even sent up to DRS a CCS according to the nature of the wound. The first stretcher case arrived at 3.30 AM. With the exception of 2 all the wounded were on S & A.M. (44 in all) The wounded on the whole were very slight, most being caused by trench mortars. There were only 2 serious cases, & both of them were G.S.W. Two cookie cars were kept at the ADS & MDS, the remainder to evacuate all cases without any delay whatsoever. Horse transport was employed by OC 41st Div Train, who expressed satisfaction with the turn out. Capt T.F. CORKILL relieved Capt W.M. BIDEN at the ADS	
	5/12/16		Capt BIDEN reported for duty here	

Army Form C. 2118

WAR DIARY
or
INTELLIGENCE SUMMARY
(Erase heading not required.)

Place	Date	Hour	Summary of Events and Information	Remarks and references to Appendices
	5/12/16		Major J.F. CROMBIE R.A.M.C. T.F. reported him to 6th Command of 139th Field Amb.	
	6/12/16		Capt S.S. CROSSE R.A.M.C. reported here for duty.	
	7/12/16		2hr 139 Inf Bgy to our fronts assigned as follows	
			10th Bn Queens — Right Subsector	
			21st Bn KRRC — Left Subsector	
			32nd Bn R.F. — RIDGEWOOD	
			26th Bn R.F. — LA CLYTTE	
	8/12/16		A.D.M.S. inspected Field Ambulances & Main Dressing Station	R.L.O

Army Form C. 2118

WAR DIARY
or
INTELLIGENCE SUMMARY
(Erase heading not required.)

Instructions regarding War Diaries and Intelligence Summaries are contained in F.S. Regs., Part II. and the Staff Manual respectively. Title Pages will be prepared in manuscript.

Place	Date	Hour	Summary of Events and Information	Remarks and references to Appendices
Shut 28 N 7 b 1.4	9/10/16	9 A.M.	Men employed as usual. Three reinforcements R.A.M.C. arrived today	
	10/10		Lt. H.F. Watson R.A.M.C. (T.C.) reported has arrived today. J.F.C.	
			Lt. Watson proceeded for duty with the 19th Hobbs Rifles.	
	11/10		Capt W.R. Brown is attached the strength. This day Roving up the men to effort for duty with to D.D.M.S. HAVRE.	
	12/10		Stretching party at R.A.P. at VEERSTRAAT increased by 15 men. Visited R.A.P. & A.D.S.	
	13/10		Lt. Watson returned to duty with this unit one can of enchu-mural transport to three [trench feet admitted	
	14/10	9 A.M.	Work as usual	
		9 P.M.	New minutes from 12th Brigade:— "Heavy bombardment of the front line trenches A.A.A. be prepared for casualties." Guns had made a trench raid on the left verbal enquiries to my Admlars, one patient of 2 Hallo higher to A.D.S. J.F. Crombie Lt Col R.A.M.C. O.C. No 139 F. Amb.	

1875. Wt. W593/826 1,000,000 4/15 J.B.C. & A. A.D.S.S./Forms/C. 2118.

WAR DIARY or INTELLIGENCE SUMMARY

Army Form C. 2118

Place	Date	Hour	Summary of Events and Information	Remarks and references to Appendices
Sheet 28 N.7.B.1.4	15th	2.30 A.M.	First Antwerp from Trenches arrived wounded.	
		midday	2.5 wounded have been admitted since 2.30 A.M. one of whom died in the Field Ambulance. 16 lying & 9 sitting. Men employed on various fatigues — new carpenters' shop erected.	
	16th		Routine work — new kitchen being enlarged, new one for patients built & room standing improvis. J.T.C.	
	17th		J.T.C. St Rehan gone to 2 Army Hygiene School. Work as usual.	
	18th		Horses inspected by Lieut-Col Lommanda this morning who approved his auto position of their condition & turnout. J.T.C.	
	19th		Lieut. Greenon R.A.M.C. (T.C.) reported to unit for duty. J.T.C.	
	20th		Infection of gas helmets on return &c. J.T.C.	
	21st to 23rd		Routine work — nothing to report. J.F. Crombie Lt Col RAMC D.C. No 139 F Amb	

Army Form C. 2118

WAR DIARY
or
INTELLIGENCE SUMMARY
(Erase heading not required.)

Instructions regarding War Diaries and Intelligence Summaries are contained in F.S. Regs., Part II. and the Staff Manual respectively. Title Pages will be prepared in manuscript.

Place	Date	Hour	Summary of Events and Information	Remarks and references to Appendices
Shut T28 A9 C 1.1	24.VIII	Noon	Hospital inspected by D.O.C. 1st Division J.T.C.	
	25/12		Observed a holiday as far as possible — extra duty employed to return supplies to B.R.C.S. J.T.C. hub & arty. Still putting dugouts &c. trench came felt than of holiday & orders issued. J.T.C.	
	26/12		Stables inspected — saw north field's cement & brickwork being carried out. J.T.C. Drainage of grounds being carried out J.T.C.	
	27/12		Visited A.D.S. & the Brasserie — work at Brasserie progressing very slowly gas shelf & inspection of latrines. Both returns & sewer retests J.T.C. Lecture R.A.M.C. (T.O.) left to talk on advance & medical chap of 18 & 19 J.T.C.	
	28/12		Left Lecture R.A.M.C. (T.O.) left to talk on advance & medical chap of 18 & 19 J.T.C.	
	29/12		Routine work — Company Sergt. of 3.D.A.D.C. arrived 2 P.	
	30/12		Half light at further & inspection for recruits & eye, slight damage to garage a half shell fell close to A.O.S. this afternoon doing slight damage (C. carried out)	
	31/12		Routine & new construction work being carried out. J.T. Burke Ft. Lt. R.A.M.C. O.C. 139 Field Amb.	

140/943.

Vol 9

41st Div.

Confidential

War Diary

139th Field Ambulance

From
Jan 1st 1917

To
Jan 31st 1917

COMMITTEE FOR THE
MEDICAL HISTORY OF THE WAR
Date 13 MAR. 1917

Army Form C. 2118

WAR DIARY
or
INTELLIGENCE SUMMARY

(Erase heading not required.)

Instructions regarding War Diaries and Intelligence Summaries are contained in F.S. Regs., Part II. and the Staff Manual respectively. Title Pages will be prepared in manuscript.

Place	Date	Hour	Summary of Events and Information	Remarks and references to Appendices
N7C 3,5 1/7 Sheet 28			Routine work being carried out & various improvements to ground, making new roads, repairing my of stable, cementing floor of Kitchens & getting them into table &c. Juncho of right rests with Enemy shells in evenings – 9 casualties brought to hour heavy shelling between 11 & 12 p.m. Distribution of Unit as follows:-	
			Main Body, 6 Lt (ZYTTE) 6 off. 2 B.N.C.O.S. 79 Men (2 N.C.O.S + 16 Men to Ren. & Supp. Coy)	
			VIERSTRATT A.D.S. 2 off. 1 N.C.O. 12 Men.	
			" " Working Party 1 " 16 "	
			R.A.P. " 1 " 25 "	
			" " (Bricks) 1 6 "	
			YPRES " " 6	
			BRASSERIE, Trolley Fatigue 1	
			att'd to A.D.M.S. 41st Div. (Riflemen) 1	
			" " 41 D.H. Train. (Wagon orderly) 1	
			Men to to Rafflete Stretcher beat. 3	
			Water Wardens, O.B. Men attached 1	
			BRASSERIE	
			RIDGE WOOD 1	
				J.J. Crosby H Capt RAMC O/C No 139 F.Amb

WAR DIARY
or
INTELLIGENCE SUMMARY
(Erase heading not required.)

Army Form C. 2118

Place	Date	Hour	Summary of Events and Information	Remarks and references to Appendices
N7C3,5 Sheet 28	2/7	10AM	General fatigues & routine front. Hospital has now been whitewashed & surgery commenced today. Sergt Othen R.A.M.C. left for England to take a commission.	
	3/7	2p.m.	Visits A.D.S. — only two trench fittings complete today. J.T.C.	J.T.C.
			Routine work — Report Dpty R.A.M.S. S.R. attached the holding rooms. J.T.C.	J.T.C.
	4/7		Inventory taken of our stores & of all stores in R.A.Ps & A.D.S. 20 R.D.41.	
			Capt GRIERSON taken over medical charge temporarily of 1	J.T.C.
	5/7	11A.M.	Conference at Office of A.D.M.S.	
		5p.m.	Vacated billett in Rome W. of Hospital — men accommodated in Hospital dugouts. Having had slight shelling between 12 noon & 5 p.m. 5 shells J.T.C.	
			My Orderly Stroh was wounded from shell fire.	
	6/7		Routine work - Infantry stand for [?] ambulance water carts e working and road made to trenches from Green road.	J.T.C.
	4/7/3 4/7/6		Routine work - clipping horses & no [?] admitted of or [?] 1/7	J.T.C.

J.F. [Crumbly?]
Lt. Col. R.A.M.C.

WAR DIARY
INTELLIGENCE SUMMARY

Army Form C. 2118

Place	Date	Hour	Summary of Events and Information	Remarks and references to Appendices
VYC&S ShT 28	10/7	9 AM	Work as usual	
	6/7		Heavy bombardment by both sides. Ford van now detailed to new R.A.P. at VEERSTRAAT to assist in bringing out wounded to A.D.S. Horses now being shifted for first time from Lieut. Philiam to A.D.S. for grazing. J.T.B.	
	11/7		Capt. Boykin R.A.M.C. returned from A.D.S.	
	12/7		Distribution of unit as follows: MAIN PARTY at M.D.S. — Officers 4. O.R. 93 Working Party " " 3. " 21 A.D.S. " 1. " 31 R.A.P. " 1. " 12 at A.D.S. R.A.P. 1 " 7 " BRASSERIE 1 " 4 VEERSTRAAT 3 " 7 Details attached, with mes— " 1 " 9 Waiting to complete. Visits A.D.S. — Hostile shelling with shrapnel. J.T. Cumbing ?/Lt. Col. R.A.M.C. O.C. 139 F.A.	

Army Form C. 2118

WAR DIARY
or
INTELLIGENCE SUMMARY
(Erase heading not required.)

Instructions regarding War Diaries and Intelligence Summaries are contained in F.S. Regs., Part II. and the Staff Manual respectively. Title Pages will be prepared in manuscript.

Place	Date	Hour	Summary of Events and Information	Remarks and references to Appendices
Shot 20 N9 C.S.S.	13/7		Weather very hot & sunny during first three days. Two crews of trench put a smoke on screen to the right & the bomblets crew of trench put 5.0.2 reinforcements arriving.	
			Capt SWINBORNE reported his arrival for duty. Left for a fortnight's contract leave.	L.T.C.
	14/7		Lieut Milton R.A.M.C. takes over permanent medical charge of 20 D&I vice Capt Gummer who returns to this ambulance for duty & relieves Lt. Milton at the A.D.S. the M.A.C. Cars who it have been permanently attached have on few wounded & evacuation in future to be carried out by the M.A.C. cars calling every morning or receipt of message stating the number of cases.	
	15/7		D.D.M.S. X 10 Corps visits ambulance today to inspect into proposed sea lines. Camps. Half unit being further today by their civilians & Cease to do [inspections?]	
			Lieut field R.A.M.C. & 10 Queens & temporary ordered [illegible] was left with the unit further on to A.D.S. vice Capt Gummer R.A.M.C.	
	16/7		Lieut Scott R.A.M.C. to A.D.S. vice Capt Gummer R.A.M.C.	J.T. Gumbie Lt. Col. R.A.M.C. O.C. 139 F.A.

WAR DIARY or INTELLIGENCE SUMMARY

Army Form C. 2118

Place: Sheet 28 N.Y.C 3.5

Date	Hour	Summary of Events and Information	Remarks and references to Appendices
17/10		Capt. Mothersmon reports here for duty from 32 R.F Royal Fusiliers & Capt. Grieson R.A.M.C. to 32 R.F. R. Kirkin as M.O. Weather dry inclement for past few days - snowing hard all today	J.T.C.
18/10		Weather still very inclement causing an increased number of sick	J.T.C.
19/10		Progress at H.Q.S. Practically nil.	J.T.C.
20/10		Has frost & very cold - range between enemy own & Allies lines converted into a quad of mud holes.	J.T.C.
21/10		Routine work.	J.T.C.
22/10		Infects now of the estimments by this own L.T.C admitted on care of Trench Fut.	
23/10 24/10		Routine work - Very severe frost. New clothing completed.	J.T.C.
		details for new old change of 2/16 A.T. by R.E. & German Prisoners of war complete	
25/10		Lt. Doyle R.A.M.C. reports has arrived for duty.	J.T.C.
26/10		Capt. M'cshannon to A.D.S. in place of Capt. White & sends Lt Doyle to include at change of 2/16 A.T. by R.E. & German prisoners of war.	J.T.C.
27/10		Lt. Col. CROMBIE went on leave	
28/10		Capt. R.L. T. M'Fay returned to Ambulance from D.K.R. & took over command of ambulance	

1875 Wt. W593/826 1,000,000 4/15 J.B.C. & A. A.D.S.S./Forms/C. 2118.

Army Form C. 2118

WAR DIARY
or
INTELLIGENCE SUMMARY
(Erase heading not required.)

Instructions regarding War Diaries and Intelligence Summaries are contained in F. S. Regs., Part II. and the Staff Manual respectively. Title Pages will be prepared in manuscript.

Place	Date	Hour	Summary of Events and Information	Remarks and references to Appendices
	29/1/17		Capt. SWINBURNE returned from leave. Lieut. DOYLE went to A.D.S. for duty.	
	30/1/17		Routine Work	
	31/1/17		Capt. R.L. Duffy attended Conference of C.O's Amb. at A.D.M.S. Office	

R.L. Duffy
Capt.
a/O.C. 1st Cav. Field Amb.
31/1/17

140/2042

War Diary

Confidential
War Diary
139th Field Ambulance

Vol 10

COMMITTEE FOR THE
MEDICAL HISTORY OF THE WAR
Date 11 MAY.1917

To
2/2/17

Feb 1917

From
1/2/17

WAR DIARY
or
INTELLIGENCE SUMMARY
(Erase heading not required.)

Army Form C. 2118

Place	Date	Hour	Summary of Events and Information	Remarks and references to Appendices
Shot 28 N7 Ch.3	1/7/17 to 4/7/17		Routine work	
	5/7/17		Lieut DOYLE went to HAZEBROUCK to School of Instruction	
			Capt McDONALD took over charge of A.D.S.	
			LIEUT WILLIAMSON returned from A.D.S. Em.D.S.	
	6/7/17		LIEUT WILLIAMSON left for England on 14 days contract leave	
	7/7/17		Lt. Col. J.F. Crombie returned from leave.	J.F.C.
	8/7/17		Routine work - men bathing - very hard front 20-25°, unable to erect tents a do much outdoor work	J.F.C.
	9/7/17		Visited front line trenches of right section, R.A.P. & A.D.S. at VEER STRAAT attended at office A.D.S. with Capt. Sunderson R.A.M.C.	J.F.C.
	10/7/17		Lieut Doyle returned from 2nd Army School of Instruction	

J.F. Crombie Lt Col. R.A.M.C.
O.C. 139 F. Amb.

Army Form C. 2118

WAR DIARY
or
INTELLIGENCE SUMMARY
(Erase heading not required.)

Instructions regarding War Diaries and Intelligence Summaries are contained in F.S. Regs, Part II. and the Staff Manual respectively. Title Pages will be prepared in manuscript.

Place	Date	Hour	Summary of Events and Information	Remarks and references to Appendices
Sheet 28 N7 C.4.3	11/2/17		Distribution of Unit. Man. Party M.D.S. Nr 6. O.P. 118 Working in A.D.S. 20 H.D.S. 13 R.A.P. 4 BRASSERIE 11	
	12/2/17		Capt Rushworth left for the line & struck off strength accordingly. Shows common cold. Thawing all day - all M.T. vehicles being washed & cleaned.	J.T.C.
	13/2/17		Freezing again - Capt Rushall R.A.M.C. to Hants Regt. for temporary duty.	J.T.C.
	14/2/17		Inspection of Sm arms - helmets & & gas shell - Frezzing.	J.T.C.
	15/2/17		Routine work - visits A.D.S. - new kitchen progressing very slowly; not a pleasant job.	J.T.C.
	16/2/17		Inspection of A.S.C. M.T. vehicles, harness & much.	J.T.C.
	17/2/17		New instructions infused. Patients hospital imagines for stores & furnishing tent & for 5 bedsteads. Completed arrangements for washing & drying clothes & linen.	J.T.C.

J. T. Crombie, Lt. Col. R.A.M.C.
O.C. 139 Field Amb.

Army Form C. 2118

WAR DIARY
or
INTELLIGENCE SUMMARY
(Erase heading not required.)

Place	Date	Hour	Summary of Events and Information	Remarks and references to Appendices
N?Ch3	18/7/17		Nursing Orderlies sent by enemy of front & went trenches hits by 1 & 24 Infy.	
			Thom K-1st Bn. of 17 O.R. onwards.	J.T.C.
	19/7/17		Total casualties to noon of 18th, 9 killed, 33 wounded, 3 shell shock. Inspected MURRUMBIDGEE Camp	J.T.C.
	20/7/17		Routine work - wrote Margene for stores. Case of "Shell Shock" died.	J.T.C.
	21/7/17		Visited A.D.S. R.A.P. & Trenches.	J.T.C.
	22/7/17		Routine work - inspection of the infantry in & fire drill.	J.T.C.
	23/7/17		Routine work.	
	24/7/17	11 A.M.	Capt. to Infy & Tunkill removing trenches V NERSTRAAT - WYSCHAETE ROAD	appendix I
		9 P.M.	Hospital cleared of patients, infantry to a trench said by 10th "Hunny"	Junction orders
			R.W. Suny Rept - 12th Infantry Brigade Order, no 95 - J.F.C.	appendix II
			For quietness v. appendix I, for reports being v. appendix II	refers to staffs medical arrangements

WAR DIARY or INTELLIGENCE SUMMARY

Army Form C. 2118

Place	Date	Hour	Summary of Events and Information	Remarks and references to Appendices
N7 C W 3 Shut 28 Belgium	25/2/17		Left Wulverghem after his Affiliated Coys there to hour totally [evacuated] admitted - Dis-charged.	
	26/2/17		Officers, 7 - Other ranks, 13h. Prisoners of war 2. = 143 7 am hour to midnight. Officers #1, other ranks 16 = 229 17. Men employed cleaning camp & hospital J.T.C. Routine work - Visited A.D.S. & R.A.P. Kitchen at A.D.S. J.T.C. nearly completed	
	27/2/17		Capt. Duffy R.A.M.C. Left for England to report to War Office for Service in East Africa	
	28/2/17		Routine work - New latering place for horses constructed, weekly inspection of men, returns &c + arm inspection held J.T. Cunningham. Lt. Col. R.A.M.C. O.C. 139 Field Amb.	

Appendix # I

Medical Arrangements by O.C. 139th Field Ambulance
in connection with 124th Infantry Brigade Order No 45.

1. **General Idea.**   The 10th Batt" "The Queens" R.W. Surrey Regt will carry out a raid by daylight on the enemy's trenches in the HOLLANSCHESCHOOR SALIENT at about 5 p.m on 24th February.

2. **Regimental Arrangements.**   It is understood that the Regimental Medical arrangements are being made by 124th Brigade. They are briefly as follows:—

   The Regimental Medical Officer & Stretcher Bearers will accompany the Battalion to our front line trenches.

   Twenty-four regimental stretcher bearers will accompany the attacking parties.

   The Regimental M.O. with 24 reserve Regimental Stretcher Bearers will remain in the front line trench probably in the mine shaft at the end of POPPY LANE.

   He will have with him 24 blankets & 12 extra stretchers with a supply of dressings.

   Until it is dark the wounded stretcher cases will be brought back to our front line trench and accommodated in existing bee-hive dugouts.

   As soon as it is dark the Regimental Medical Officer and reserve Stretcher Bearers will proceed to a point A just behind the old breastworks about 30 yards on the S.W side of the VIERSTRAAT- WYTSCHAETE Road and about 50 yards behind our front line trench.

   All stretcher cases will be brought to this point where they will be taken over by the Field Ambulance Bearers.   This point A will be in telephonic communication with point B on the VIERSTRAAT SWITCH

5. At the Advanced Dressing Station there will be two Medical Officers and 12 men.
Capt: IMPEY. R.A.M.C. S.R. in charge.

There will be stationed here a reserve of one N.C.O and 16 Stretcher Bearers with 4 stretchers.

A reserve of 18 long stretchers is at the A.D.S.

Cases will be evacuated from here to the Main Dressing Station in Divisional cars.

6. Walking Wounded.
Walking wounded will proceed via POPPY LANE to the New Regimental Aid Post at N11a5.3. Sheet 28, 1-20,000.

One Medical Officer, 4 Stretcher Bearers and 4 Nursing Orderlies will be stationed at this Aid Post.

From here the walking wounded will be directed down the road past the Advanced Dressing Station to the BARDENBURGH ESTAMINET at the Cross Roads at N3 d 5.5. whence they will be conveyed to the Main Dressing Station by Motor or horse transport.

7. One N.C.O. & one man will be stationed at the BARDENBURGH ESTAMINET to superintend the loading of the walking wounded.

8. Transport.
One Motor Ambulance will be stationed at the A.D.S.

Four large Motor Ambulances and two horsed Ambulances will be stationed on the road about 50 yards W.S.W. of the BARDENBURGH ESTAMINET at N3 d. 4. 6. Sheet 28, 1-20,000.

Moribund   No Moribund case is to be evacuated to
cases.   the Casualty Clearing Station.

13 Medical   The Quartermaster will arrange for an extra
Comforts.   supply of Medical Comforts ie R.A.P, A.D.S, and
                 M.D.S.

22-2-1917.

                                                           Crombie
                                                   Lt. Col. R.A.M.C.
                                        O.C. 139 Field Ambulance

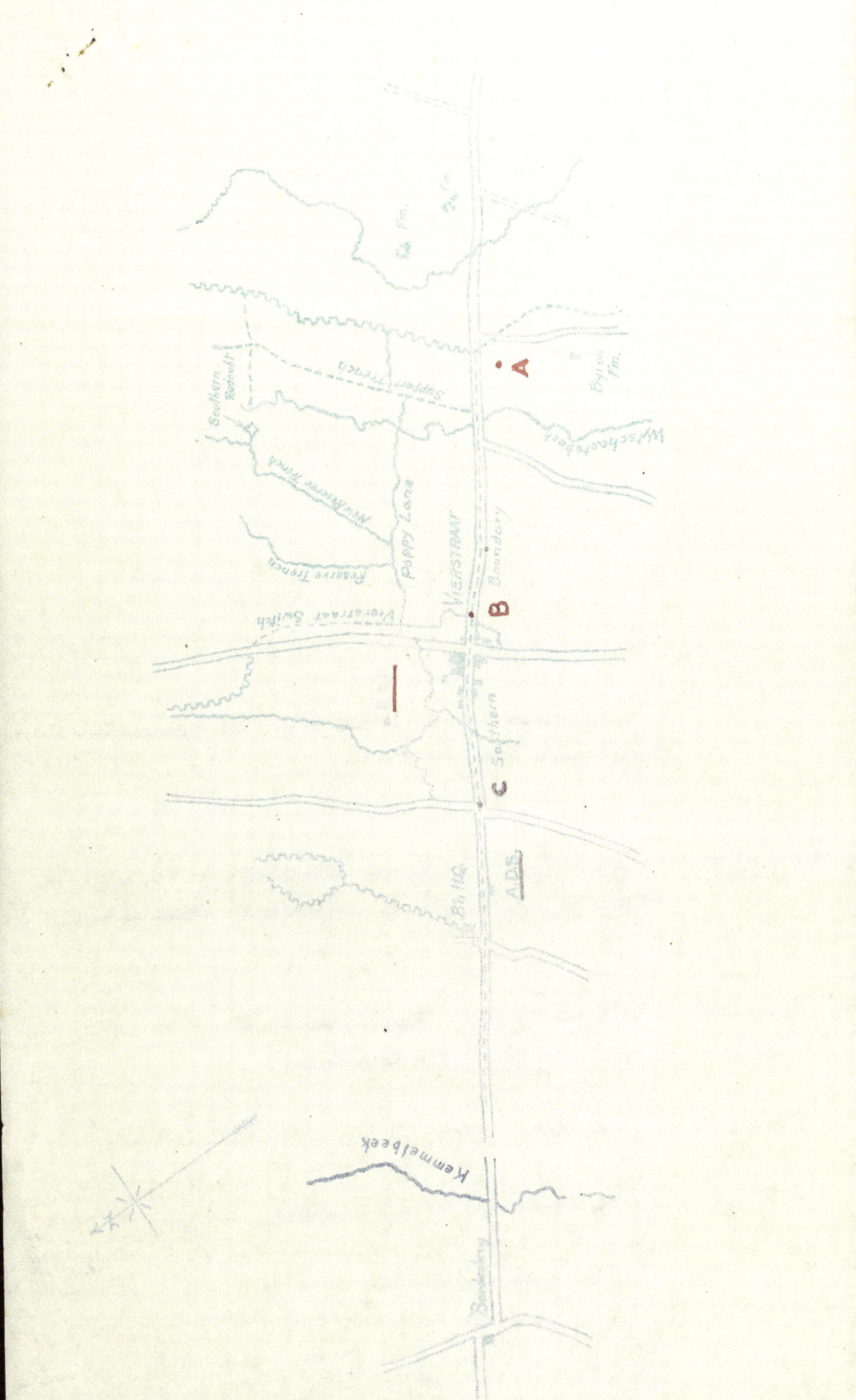

Appendix II
1

Report on the arrangements made for the evacuation of wounded in connection with operations by 124th Infantry Brigade on the night of Feby 24/25. 1917.

The advanced arrangements were as follows, Capt: Impey R.A.M.C. in charge.

(a) At the A.D.S, Capts: Impey & Elliott with 13 other ranks and 17 reserve Stretcher Bearers.

(b) At VIERSTRAAT 15 other ranks with 7 Wheeled Stretchers.

(c) In the VIERSTRAAT SWITCH close to the VIERSTRAAT-WYTSCHAETE Road, Capt: Corkill, R.A.M.C. with 42 Stretcher Bearers.

(d) At the VIERSTRAAT R.A.P. Capt: Roach R.A.M.C. with 7 other ranks.

(e) At the BRASSERIE 15 other ranks.

TRANSPORT. At the A.D.S. one large Motor Ambulance, and at the Cross Roads at BRANDENBURGH 4 large Motor Ambulances, and 2 Horsed Ambulances.

WALKING WOUNDED. All walking wounded were evacuated via POPPY LANE to the R.A.P. where they were dressed and directed past the A.D.S. to the BRANDENBURGH Cross Roads where one N.C.O and one Private R.A.M.C. were stationed to superintend their loading on Motor or Horse Ambulances, whichever happened to be available.

MAIN DRESSING STATION.

At the Main Dressing Station arrangements were as on attached plan.

The C.O. with Capts: Swinburne & Royle R.A.M.C. were at the M.D.S. and 10 other ranks A.S.C. H.T. were responsible for loading and unloading the Ambulances.

DIARY.

4-30 p.m. Hospital at M.D.S. empty, and ready for the reception of cases.

Capt: Impey R.A.M.C. reported all advanced parties in position.

4-55 p.m. Artillery bombardment started.

5-30 p.m. First walking wounded reached A.D.S.

5-50 p.m. First Stretcher case reached A.D.S.

6-0 p.m. Everything ready at M.D.S.

6-20 p.m. Walking wounded arrived at M.D.S. in Motor Ambulance.

7-0 p.m. First Stretcher case reached M.D.S.

6-30 p.m. Capt: Corkill, R.A.M.C. with Stretcher Bearers went to front line trench, got in touch with Capt: Todd R.A.M.C. M.O./c 10th Queens and proceeded to evacuate all lying wounded from the front line.

7-15 p.m. All reserve bearers sent to R.A.P. to cope with a rush that occurred there.

This was largely due to the fact that many severely wounded men, including one man with a penetrating abdominal wound, managed to walk down POPPY LANE as far as the R.A.P. and there had to be converted into stretcher cases.

8.30 p.m. Hostile artillery fire practically ceased.
10-30 p.m. Last case evacuated from the R.A.P. and all reserve Stretcher Bearers sent up to the front line to assist Capt: Corkill.
11-30 p.m. All cases collected from the front line by Capts: Corkill & Todd.
1-30 a.m. All the Stretcher cases were in the A.D.S. by 1-30 a.m. with the exception of two on the extreme left of the line, which had to be carried down POPPY LANE.

At the M.D.S. there was a steady stream of wounded up till 2.a.m, but at no time any congestion, all cases being evacuated by No 11. M.A.C. as soon as they had been dressed and had warm food.

The largest number in the Hospital at one time was at 11-15 p.m, when there were 7 lying and 17 walking wounded.

Cases dealt with up to midnight were Officers, 5. other ranks 119, prisoners of war 2.

At 2-15 a.m. the Hospital was clear until 2-30 a.m, thereafter, cases arrived up till 6-15 a.m.

All arrangements worked without a hitch, 120 cases being evacuated from the A.D.S. in 6 hours.

The success of the evacuation was very largely
due to the excellent organising power of
Capt: Corkill, R.A.M.C., and his gallant leading
of his Bearer Section.

Number of casualties dealt with :-
Officers 7. Other Ranks 134. Prisoners of War 2.
Of these 63 were lying cases.

Fully 95% of these were shell wounds and
fully 50% of these appeared to be shrapnel.

Many of the walking cases were only slightly
wounded and should soon be fit for duty again.

The only trouble experienced was in connection
with the Road from the A.D.S. to the
BRANDENBURGH Cross Roads.
Owing to the frost and the heavy traffic of the
previous night this road cut up very badly.
It was specially bad at the lower end near
the Cross Roads; here the mud was over a foot
deep and Ambulances could only get through
with difficulty assisted by a fatigue party and
a horse from the Field Ambulance.
One Motor Ambulance was bogged for two
hours and another could not be got out
till next morning.

The axle of one of the Bruce MacCormac
stretcher carriages got bent — This is the weak
spot of these carriages as similar trouble has
been previously experienced with them.

The Regimental arrangements were made by the 124th Brigade.

Twenty four Stretcher Bearers followed after the raiding party, and another 24 with 12 spare stretchers & blankets remained under the charge of the Regimental Medical Officer.
These were scattered along the front line trench and consequently touch was lost with them when they were required for searching No Man's Land after the raid.

If tactical reasons admit, I would suggest these reserve Stretcher Bearers should, if possible, be kept together at some central point till required.

There are no further suggestions to make, except that a much larger number of stomach warmers should be issued to Field Ambulances. Many of the cases were cold and collapsed, and the cars of No. 11. M.A.C. are not heated.

J. F. Crombie
Lt. Col. R.A.M.C. (T)
O.C. 139 Field Amb.

26-2-17

Main Dressing Station.

Plan of
Arrangements for the Night of February 24th & 25th 1917

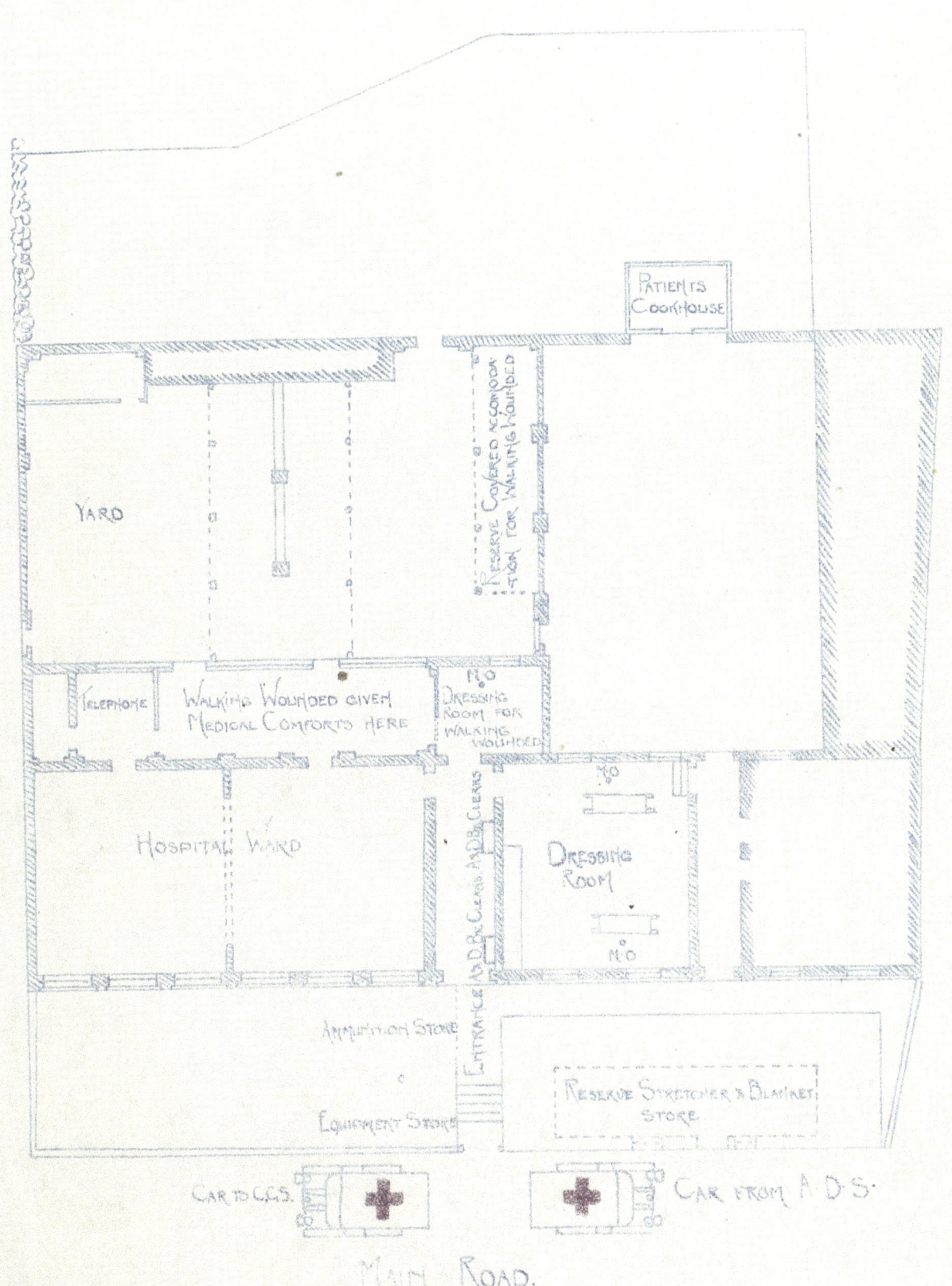

Confidential 140/2042
War Diary 41st Div.
139th Field Ambulance

Vol XI

From
1st March 1917
To
31st March 1917

COMMITTEE FOR THE
MEDICAL HISTORY OF THE WAR
Date 11 MAY 1917

WAR DIARY or INTELLIGENCE SUMMARY

(Erase heading not required.)

Army Form C. 2118

Place	Date	Hour	Summary of Events and Information	Remarks and references to Appendices
N7 c 4.3 Sheet 28 Belgium 1-40,000	1/3/17		Capt. J.S. Doyle returned to 2¹ K.R.R.R. for temporary duty. Working Party of 40 men sent to BRANDENBURG Cnr roads to where the road from there to the A.D.S. Ypres road is now impassable till lying save have to be brought in wheeled stretchers from the A.D.S. to the Cnr roads. Distribution — M.D.S. Offr 3 — O.R. 28. " A.D.S. " 1 " 14 VIERSTRAAT RAP " ― " 4 BRASSERIE working Party " 20 BRANDENBURG working Party 40 Details " 5 Officers attached 4	J.F. Campbell Lt Col. R.A.M.C. O.C. 139 Field Amb.

WAR DIARY or INTELLIGENCE SUMMARY

Army Form C. 2118

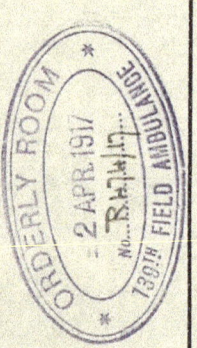

Place	Date	Hour	Summary of Events and Information	Remarks and references to Appendices
N7 C.b.3 Knut's D Bulford H.Q. ore	2/3/17		Capt. GORFUNKEL R.A.M.C. reports his arrival from Infantry Bn. Routine work.	J.T.C.
	3/3/17		Visited A.D.S. RIDGE WOOD & BRASSERIE	J.T.C.
	4/3/17		Routine work — Work party still on Rds from BRANDENBURGH to A.D.S.	J.T.C.
	5/3/17		Inspection & upkeep in camp of 016 G.A.T.R.E. & Prisoners of War camp.	J.T.C.
	6/3/17		Routine work — Inclement weather with snow & frost interfering with ordinary work. Refurnished road to A.D.S. from BRANDENBURGH stopping	
	7/3/17		owing to thaw. A.D.S. from Rds & fireplace being built. New kitchen at A.D.S.	J.T.C.
	8/3/17		Pte. (A/Sgt.) NORRIS F. & Pte. AKHURST J.L. awarded the Military Medal for gallantry in the field. A.D.M.S. order no.D/8-3-17.	J.T.C.
	9/3/17		Routine work — working in Rear standings & stores for Motor ambulance	J.T.C.
	10/3/17			
	11/3/17		O.D.M.S. IX Corps visited M.D.S. & A.D.S. Weather improves	J.T.C.
	12/3/17			

J.T. Crumbie
Lt. R.A.M.C.

WAR DIARY or INTELLIGENCE SUMMARY

(Erase heading not required.)

Army Form C. 2118

Place	Date	Hour	Summary of Events and Information	Remarks and references to Appendices
Sheet 28 1:40,000 N7c.3	13/3/17		A.D.M.S. visits Ambulance. A.D.S. & R.A.P.'s. Standing of Motor Ambulances completed.	J.F.C.
	14/3/17		Capt. Swinburne R.A.M.C. (T.C.) left the unit to report to D.D.M.S. ROUEN. Lieut. E. ASHBY R.A.M.C. (T.C.) joins from ROUEN.	J.F.C.
	15/3/17		Moving hut to B at VIERSTRAAT disinterment. All equipment being sorted out - checks & repaires - Tents stowed &c. J.F.C. Preparing to move hut to next area.	J.F.C.
	16/3/17		Capt. McD.G. MOLLOY R.A.M.C. reports his arrival for duty from 2nd/1st RE. Lieut i Ashby R.A.M.C. proceeds to Capt. from 5-3-17 & left this unit. Sent South via R.E.	J.F.C.
	17/3/17		Wagons being packed &c.	J.F.C.
	18/3/17		Brethren Mark. moves to tell 6 at STEENVOORDE	J.F.C.
	19/3/17		"	
	20/3/17		Inclement weather - Sleet & rain. Advanced party sent to STEENVOORDE. 1 Offr + 100 O.Ranks. of 587 mt Runners at 5 p.m.	J.F. Cumphries R.A.M.C. M.C. O.C. 139 Field Amb.

WAR DIARY
or
INTELLIGENCE SUMMARY

Army Form C. 2118

Place	Date	Hour	Summary of Events and Information	Remarks and references to Appendices
Sheet 28 1.40,000 N 7 b 4.3	21/3/17	12 noon	Handed over H.D.S. to No 58 F. Amb together with Quar, B.R.C.S & other stores & wares the remainy recip6	
		1.30 p.m	Main body left for STEENVORDE for training. Weather very inclement	
Sheet 27 NE 1.20,000 R 31, C.2.1	22/3/17		Hospital Infans at No 3 Rue de POPERINGHE, STEENVORDE Office at 7 Rue de CARNOT. Transport lines 1 mile W.	
	23/3/17		Training — Three parades & a Lecture. Weather inclement, no training ground available	
	24/3/17		" " " . Weather inclement - training ground too wet to use.	
	25/3/17		Church Parade & Rest day.	
	26/3/17		Very wet - three parades & a lecture. three lines very muddy & wet.	
	27/3/17		Training, very wet day	
	28/3/17		" " " " "	
	29/3/17 30/3/17 31/3/17		Training — weather inclement	

J. F. Crawfurd Lt Col R.A.M.C.
O.C. 139 F. Amb.

Medical
April 1917

No 7026

Vol 12

Confidential.

War Diary

139th Field Ambulance

R.A.M.C.

COMMITTEE FOR THE
MEDICAL HISTORY OF THE WAR
Date -6 JUN.1917

To :-
30th April 1917

From :-
1st April 1917

139th Field Ambulance

WAR DIARY or INTELLIGENCE SUMMARY

Army Form C. 2118

Place	Date	Hour	Summary of Events and Information	Remarks and references to Appendices
STEENVOORDE	1/4/17		Military models presented to L/Cpl. NORRIS & Pte. AKHURST by G.O.C. 41st Division.	
	2/4/17		Rest day — very inclement weather. Study of day tactical scheme & establishment of advanced main dressing stations	
	3/4/17		Tactical scheme with Brigade. Stretchers carrying to Snowstorm. Lectures & route march substituted.	
	4/4/17		Tactical route march by sections.	
	5/4/17		Working party of 1 Offr & 50 O.R. under Lieut. Postill R.A.M.C. sent to A.D.S. DICKEBUSCH. Advanced party under Lieuts. Wilkinson & Buchanan sent to take over 140 Fd. Amb. D.R.S. Questions asked, taken for also further & splendid ws. 1, 2, 3.	Question: Order no 2 offenders? Order for prophylact of offenders & orders for digging party offenders. 3
	6/4/17		Took over 41st Divisional Rest Station at 12-30 P.M. & Transport at 3 P.M. Taking over certificate signed. Personnel arrived at 12-30 P.M. J.F. Crombie Lt Col R.A.M.C. O.C. 139 Field Amb.	

WAR DIARY
or
INTELLIGENCE SUMMARY
(Erase heading not required.)

Army Form C. 2118

Place	Date	Hour	Summary of Events and Information	Remarks and references to Appendices
Sheet 27 N.E. Belgium I.20.d.45 L.28.d.5.5	7/4/17		Busy organising & cleaning D.R.S.	
	8/4/17		M^r i/c of A. Section take charge of all motor work, sanitation, evacuation work " " B " " " " " Medical Wards " " C " " " " " " " " E " " " " " Surgical Wards	
	9/4/17		Two ambulances, motors, with orderlies attached for the night to 47th Division	
	10/4/17		Routine work	
	11/4/17		" "	
	12/4/17		" " D.R.S. visited by 9r hoods Hutchison from America	
	13/4/17		Routine work	
	14/4/17 9 AM		" " Two loads of bricks from YPRES A.D.M.S. inspected camp & arrangements for P.B. &	
	15/4/17		Number of Patients 234. Empty beds 86 " 47 " " " 233 " " 47	

J.J. Crombie
LT. COL. R.A.M.C.
O.C. 139 Field Amb.

WAR DIARY or INTELLIGENCE SUMMARY

Army Form C. 2118

ORDERLY ROOM
30 APR. 1917
No. 561
139th FIELD AMBULANCE

Place	Date	Hour	Summary of Events and Information	Remarks and references to Appendices
Sheet 27 N.E. Belgium 1/20,000	16/4/17	9 A.M.	Total number of patients, 232	
		10.30	O.9.M.S. X 1st Corps visits D.R.S.	
4.28.d.3.5	17/4/17	9 A.M.	Routine work. Total number of patients — 220 J.T.C.	
	18/4/17		Number of patients — 196.	
	19/4/17		Read by A.D.M.S. — number of patients in D.R.S. 176	
			One private of working party wounded & evacuated to C.C.S.	
			One private of working party wounded & evacuated to C.C.S.	
	20/4/17		Distribution of unit as follows	
			Main Party - D.R.S. - WIPPENHOECK -	Officers. O.R. — 119
			VORMOZEELE	5 6
			ABEELE 1. GODWAERSVELDE. 2.	3
			Data Service	7
			Command	1
			M.O/c. 10-15 Queens Leave	1
			Officer	
			Wanting to complete	8
				9 183
				J.T. Crombie Lt.Col. R.A.M.C. O.C. 139 Field Amb

WAR DIARY or INTELLIGENCE SUMMARY

Army Form C. 2118

Place	Date	Hour	Summary of Events and Information	Remarks and references to Appendices
Sheet 27 NE Belgium 1-20.b.6 L.28.d.35	21/4/17		Bentinc Avok – Patients 181 Patients 173	
	22/4/17 23/4/17	6.45 AM	Stray small shell from front – a number of the personal were affected with lachrymatory shop + some lacrymation – two minutes but all returned to duty. Friends slight found N5 and a gunner N.O.S.	
		7.15 AM	Friend symptoms + ? known any camp being clear of this 7.30 AM to not turn to have effects. By telephone it was ascertained that POPERINGHE & the C.C.S. at REMY SIDING has been similarly affected. It was at first thought to be the novelty of the shells but subsequently was found to be from a by far attack on the French at NIEUPORT, 25 miles NE Relief working party of 2 NCO's + 23 men sent to VORMEZELE, the Ruffling of these returning patients 181. Division inspected the Rent Station. G.O.C. 41st Division inspected the Rent Station. Patients 207	
	24/4/17			
	25/4/17		Patients 219. a/Sup. Return proceeded to Transportation R.E. Troops Left 11 O/c	
	26/4/17		Patients 221. Capt. S.F.Y. Elliot proceeded to 230 Roadstone Bgt. as temp M.O.C.	
	27/4/17		Patients to 234. Gas Instruction – Work Party NIPPENDEN officers 6, O.R. 113. VORMEZELE working party - O.R. 50. Water carriers 3 Boncourt 9 M.O.C 10th Division I M.O.I. 23° Roadstone I. Leave 0.1. O.R.I. To complete 6. Total of O.R. 183 J.F. Comba M.O.B. R.A.M.C. M.O C 139 Field Amb	

Army Form C. 2118

WAR DIARY
or
INTELLIGENCE SUMMARY
(Erase heading not required.)

ORDERLY ROOM
30 APR. 1917
No. S.51
139TH FIELD AMBULANCE

Place	Date	Hour	Summary of Events and Information	Remarks and references to Appendices
Sheet 27. N.E. Belgium I. 20. d. 4.28.d.3.5	28/4/17	9 A.M.	Paraded 242.	
	29/4/17	"	" 240. Party of 6 men as working party to VORMOZEELE collecting post.	
	30/4/17	"	" 227. Sgt Daniel Bowles to England to take a commission in R.F.A.	

J F Crombie
Lt Col. R.A.M.C.
O.C. 139 Field Amb.

SECRET.

Appendix 1.   Copy No 2.   War Diary
139th Field Ambulance, R.A.M.C.

Operation Order No. 2.   Copy No. 2.

[Stamp: ORDERLY ROOM 30 APR. 1917 No. S.51 139TH FIELD AMBULANCE]

1. This Field Ambulance will leave the Training Area on April 6th 1917, and will take over the charge of the Divisional Rest Station from the 140th Field Ambulance.

2. This Field Ambulance will proceed by Route March accompanied by Transport.   Head of column not to pass Road Junction K.32.d.4.0., Map 27, 1-20,000, N.E., before 6.0 p.m.

3. Blankets and waterproof sheets will be carried by transport.

4. An advance working party of 4 N.C.O's and 46 men under the Command of Capt. J. Cahill, R.A.M.C., (S.R.) will be at the A.D.S., DICKEBUSH, by 12.0 noon, April 5th.   Detailed instructions for this party are issued separately.

5. An advance party of 2 Officers, 10 N.C.O's and 32 men, under the Command of Capt. J. Williamson, R.A.M.C., will proceed to the Divisional Rest Station on the morning of April 5th.
One G.S. Wagon, 2 Water Carts, One Motor Ambulance and one motor cyclist will accompany this party. Detailed instructions are issued separately.

6. The Quartermaster will check and take over all Red Cross and Medical Stores, Medical Comforts and Area Stores from the 140th Field Ambulance, and will arrange for each party to take the unexpired portion of the day's rations and one day's rations with them.

7. All billets to be left clean — they will be inspected by the Orderly Officer who will render a report.

8. A rear party of one N.C.O. and 3 men will be left to clear up the Mess Room, Hospital, etc.

(Continued overleaf).

9/ All patients will be sent to the M.R. Station. If necessary, a rear party of one officer and 2 nursing orderlies will remain.

10/ Orders for march will be issued later.

11/ Acknowledge.

4/4/17

J. F. Crombie Lt. Col., R.A.M.C.
Commanding, 139th Field Ambulance.

Issued at 6-0 p.m.

Distribution
    Copy No. 1. File.
           2. War Diary.
           3. A.D.M.S.
           4. 124th Inf. Brigade.
           5. 140th Field Ambulance.
           6.
           to } All officers.
           16.
           17. Spare.
           18.

Appendix 2   Copy No 2.   War Diary

Secret

Orders for Advanced Working Party

[Stamp: ORDERLY ROOM / 30 APR 1917 / No. 451 / 139th FIELD AMBULANCE]

A working Party of 4+ N.C.O's and 4.6 men (including one cook) under the Command of Capt J.D Corkill R.amC 139 will proceed by march route on Thursday to A.D.S. at DICKEBUSH, to arrive there by 12-0 noon to relieve the working Party of the 140th Field Ambulance.

Capt Corkill will take over from O.C., 140th Field Ambulance Working Party, all documents and instructions relating to the work.

    Dress— Skeleton Order with groundsheet and Box Respirator
    Haversack Ration to be carried, and
    Water Bottle half-full.
Breakfast — 6-0 am.
Parade — 7-0 am.

Packs and blankets will be placed in the school yard, RUE CARNOT, before 7-0am, and one N.C.O. and the cook left as baggage guard.

They will take 4 Camp Kettles, the unexpired portion of the day's ration, one day's rations, and one day's fuel with them.

All packs, stores, etc., will be taken to Dickebush by the Sanitary Lorry which will be in Rue Carnot at 9-0 am, and will load Stores at the School yard.

Detail of Party :—

Sgt.	Cox	E.	Pte Harding R.J.	Pte. Parker S.H.
Cpl.	Fleming	E.W.	" Henderson H.	" Penellum E.
"	Ingram	W.J.	" Hamilton J.	" Payne P.J.
L/Cpl.	Norris	J.	" Kench H.M.	" Roberts H.
Pte.	Akhurst	J.M.	" Lewis J.	" Robinson J.B.
"	Bassett	J.J.(Cook)	" Memory L.	" Reynolds A.C.
"	Creighton	A.H.	" Mills S.	" Short J.
"	Cambell	W.B	" Moon J.P.	" Saunders C.E.
"	Douch	H.J.	" Mould J.E.	" Sanders W.C.
"	Evans	C.	" Munro A.	" Swinfield W.
"	Goodman	A.J.	" Moore C.E.	" Sayers G.Wm
			" Price W.	" Steele S.A.
			" Pearce J.	" Sanders J.
"	Gamblin	W.	" Prince W.	" Tanner C.W.
"	Gallagher	J.P.	" Pares W.E.	" Willis K.J.
"	Graham	A.	" Philpott H.	" Whitehouse J.S.
			" Price E.R.	" Welch J.
			" Walker H.	" Woolcott E.

.... Lt Col R.A.M.C.
Commanding 139th F.A.

Distribution
 Copy No. 1. File.
        2. War Diary
        3. A.D.M.S.
        4. Capt. J.J. Corkill, Rank
        5. Qr. Mr.   S.R.
        6. Sgt Cot.

Appendix 3   Copy No. 2. War Diary

Secret

[Stamp: ORDERLY ROOM / 30 APR 1917 / No. 851 / 139TH FIELD AMBULANCE]

An advance party of 2 officers and O.R. as noted
will parade at 9 A.M. on Monday, 30th April 1917 under
the command of Captain J.W. Wilkinson, R.A.M.C.,
by march route to near Bus House.
Dress – Marching order.

Blankets and Waterproof sheets will be carried by
horse transport. They will be struck at 8 A.M.
on the breakfast of Officers' mess. Baggage party
of one N.C.O. and two men.

Detail of Party:-
   Officers - Capt. J.W. Wilkinson, R.A.M.C.
              Capt. F.S. Buchanan, R.A.M.C.

Q.M. Sgt. Holmes, Pte. Stevens J.	Office Staff	Pte. Hill	Recreation Room
Cpl. Stilwell, Pte. Ward	Packers	Pte. Bryant, Dawber	Officers' Servants
Pte. Harris and Laybourn	Dining Hall	Pte. Smith M.D.	Officers' Mess
Cpl. Poole, Pte. Johnson	Cooks	L/Cpl. Smith, Sherratt, Hall	Clerks
Pte. Jones O.H.	Smith	Sgt. Daniels	Dispenser
Sgts. Ruthern and Bennett	Nursing	Pte. Houlger B.W.	Gardener
L/Cpl. Hocking, Ptes.		Ptes. Houlger S., Gunning	
Charnock, Longworth, Unwin		and Squires	General Duty
Spencer, Burrell, Jewitt J.,	Orderlies	Pte. Munro C.S.	Cook for School of Sanitation, Borsohepe
Jewett J.		Pte. Green acting L.S.	Water Duty Ecowarroveide
Pte. Hopkins	Disinfector	Pte. Stephenson	Water Duty Abeele
Sgt. Sucker, Pte. Watkins	Bath	One Sgt. and two	Water Duty
Pte. Drakeford	Guard	Drivers, A.S.C., A.T.	Detachment
		F.W. Essex	Water Cart Orderly

On arrival one motor ambulance and one motor cyclist will be
sent to the office of the A.D.M.S., 41st Division, to relieve
the ambulance and cyclist of the 140th Field Ambulance.

One cook (Pte. Munro C.S.) and 1 G.S. Wagon
with driver and horses with the detail to proceed to the Corps School
of Sanitation, BORSOHEPE, to relieve the vehicles and personnel
of 140th Field Ambulance.

Two Water Duty men (Ptes. GREEN A. and KING L.S.) will be
detailed for duty at water point at ECOWARROVELDE, Sheet 27 S.E.
R 2 c 8.9., and one (Pte. STEPHENSON R.) for duty at
ABEELE, Sheet 27 N.E., L 32, L.3.9.

Capt. F.S. Buchanan R.A.M.C. will take over all the out-door
work, such as sanitation, disinfector baths, recreation and
dining rooms, huts etc., and will have the working explained to
him.

(continued overleaf)

Capt. J. Williamson R.A.M.C. will take over the duties and attend the necessary details as regards nursing etc.

The A.S.Sgt. will be responsible for all stores and will if necessary in conjunct with the O.C. 140 Field Ambulance will see that an equivalent is obtained.

The sunny side section of the tent's interior and also with any rations will be carried on the transport.

J.F. Crombie Lt.Col. R.A.M.C.
Commanding 139th F.A.

4/4/17

Distribution
Copy No 1. File
2. War Diary
3. A.D.M.S.
4. 140th Field Amb.
5. Capt: J Williamson R.A.M.C.
6. Capt: G.G. Buchanan
7. Qr.mr:
8. Spare.
9.
10.
"
16

140/2/61
Vol 13

Confidential
War Diary
of
139th Field Ambulance
R.A.M.C.

From
1st May 1917
To
31st May 1917

COMMITTEE FOR THE
MEDICAL HISTORY OF THE WAR
Date 10 JUL 1917

WAR DIARY
or
INTELLIGENCE SUMMARY

Army Form C. 2118

(Erase heading not required.)

Place	Date	Hour	Summary of Events and Information	Remarks and references to Appendices
WULVERDINGHE WIPPENAOEK	May 1st to 5/5/17		Routine work	
	6/5/17		3 h patients & 2 men of the unit left for the seaside breakdown camp at ambulance	
	7/5/17		Capt. Cockhill R.A.M.C. proceeded to VORMEZEELE as O/C working party. Capt. Buchanan R.A.M.C. proceeded to 328th Royal Fusiliers as permanent M.O. Capt. M.D. Hurley proceeded on 10 days' leave to England.	
	8/5/17		Capt. Grove R.A.M.C. reported his arrival & to be attached for discipline & rations. A party of men had their gas helmets tested at the Gas school.	
	9/5/17		Capt. Baker A.C. R.A.M.C. reported his arrival for duty.	
	10/5/17		1 N.C.O. & 6 men to VORMEZEELE in relief of working party. Capt. Wilkinson R.A.M.C. to 21 K.R.R. as temp. M.O.	
	11/5/17		Routine work - settles being collected from non vegetable by patients & personnel, & from	
	12/5/17		Capt. Grove R.A.M.C. to be forty third Field amb. from the 7th instant for duty	
	13/5/17 14/5/17		Routine work	

J.T. Cumlin
Lt. Col. RAMC
OC 139 Field Amb

WAR DIARY or INTELLIGENCE SUMMARY

Army Form C. 2118

Place	Date	Hour	Summary of Events and Information	Remarks and references to Appendices
Sheet 27 1/E L28 b.7.1	15/5/17		All line infantry who with lachrymatory gas — hopes & smoke to who with respirators with mouth tubes. Capt. Ross R.A.M.C. T.C. reports his arrival for duty. — J.T.C.	
	16/17 17/17 18/5/17		Routine work.	
	19/5/17		J.T.C.	
			251 returned to D.R.S. at noon. Capt Ong R.A.M.C. proceeds to 18 K.R.R. as permanent medical officer. Capt Fifield left from R.A.M.C. who reports his arrival on posting to this field ambulance. One hospital marquee erected. J.T.C.	
	20/5/17		Returns to D.R.S. at noon, 275	J.T.C.
	21/5/17		" " " " 244	J.T.C.
	1/5 25/17		Routine work.	

J T Crumplie
Lt. Col. R.A.M.C.
O.C. 139 Field Amb.

Army Form C. 2118

WAR DIARY
or
INTELLIGENCE SUMMARY
(Erase heading not required.)

ORDERLY ROOM
31 MAY 1917
No. S.66
139TH FIELD AMBULANCE

Place	Date	Hour	Summary of Events and Information	Remarks and references to Appendices
Shut 17NE L28 b 7	26/5/17 to 30/5/17		Routine work — from 70 to 180 patients being admitted every day	J.T.C.
	31/5/17		Capt. Hadley left for temporary duty with 52 Bde A.T.A. Capt Watson WEBB & Howard PRENTISS joined for temporary duty	J T Cumbersine Lt. Col. R.A.M.C. O.C. 139 Field Amb.

24

Conf...

War Diary

139th Field Ambulance

F. of O. 16 C.

from 1/6/17 to 30/6/17

June 1917

Vol 14

Attached sheet, 1 Field Amb Summary

COMMITTEE FOR THE
MEDICAL HISTORY OF THE WAR
Date -7 AUG. 1917

Plan of D.R.S.

Withdrawn.

139 F.D. June 17

WAR DIARY or INTELLIGENCE SUMMARY

Army Form C. 2118

ORDERLY ROOM
30 JUN 1917
No. 599
139th FIELD AMBULANCE

Place	Date	Hour	Summary of Events and Information	Remarks and references to Appendices
Sheet 27 N.E.(c) L26677	1/6/17	9 AM	Returns whether Q 3 Weekly 225. Capt WEBB RAMC proceeded to 52 B Further no permanent R.O/C Distribution	
				O.R
			Bearer Party WIPPEN HOEK	7 101
			Bathing Party VORMOZELE	1 56
			Water Wanders ABEELE	— 1
			" GODWAERSVELDE	— 2
			1 (P.B) Sheet 27 L32, R6-7	— 1
			Command officer 10 CCS	— —
			M.O/c 10 Queens	— —
			" 91 K.R.R	— —
			" 52 Bde A.F.A.	— —
			" 82 Royal Fusiliers	— 16
			To complete	
				13 183
				J F Knowles Lt Col RAMC

Army Form C. 2118

WAR DIARY
or
INTELLIGENCE SUMMARY

(Erase heading not required.)

Instructions regarding War Diaries and Intelligence Summaries are contained in F.S. Regs., Part II. and the Staff Manual respectively. Title Pages will be prepared in manuscript.

Place	Date	Hour	Summary of Events and Information	Remarks and references to Appendices
Shot 17 N E 6 2/17 L 28 b 6.1	2/6/17	9 A.M.	Divisional Horse Show - entries for G.S. Wagon & Pair of Heavy Draught Horses. Patients admitted - 6 3. - Dischargers Remaining 228	
	3/6/17	9 A.M.	Patients admitted 5 h " 239	
			Capt. J. S. DARRE M.C. to 21st K.R.R.C. as M.O/C	J.T.C.
			Capt. J. S. WILLIAMSON reports his arrival from 21st R.R.R. Taken on the strength of this unit y.p.	J.T.C.
	4/6/17	9 A.M.	Patients admitted 51. Remaining 164.	
			65 Patients left for 2nd Army Sanitoile Camp at AMBLETEUSE	J.T.C.
	5/6/17	10 A.M.	Conference at A.D.M.S's office re impending operations. Capt. ROSSE R.A.M.C. reports for duty from No 10 C.C.S.	J.T.C.
	6/6/17	Noon	Operation No 3 issued. - Capt. PRENTISS R.A.M.C. proceeds on temp. M.O/c 12 E. Surrey Regt in relief of Capt. BINNIE, R.A.M.C. evacuated wounded	O.O no 3 Appendix (1)
		3-15 P.M.	Zero hour intimated	
		5.30 P.M.	2 offs + 2 bearer subdivisions proceeds to OUDERDOM to report to O/C 138 F. amb. together with 3 horse ambulances + 6 G.S. wagons for the heavy sitting cases, also in cage + 2 Ford Motor Ambulances	

War Diary or Intelligence Summary

Army Form C. 2118

ORDERLY ROOM
30 JUN. 1917
No. 599
77/34 FIELD AMBULANCE

Place	Date	Hour	Summary of Events and Information	Remarks and references to Appendices
Shirt 7N E 6/6/17 d 28, d.3.6 continued		5.30pm	Two Offrs + 1 tent subdivision proceeded to Enfr Sevens by wounded dressing station at BRAND HOEK. Were enjoined here to extend this D.R.S. to accommodate 200, it was actually extended to accommodate 550 with possible extension to 800 of regard. 10 small hospital marquees were erected giving accommodation for 200 & five bell tents. In plan of D.R.S. there are coloured red - appendix 2. All have equipped with blankets, 2 per man, + either with palliasses & pillow or the floor covered with straw + ground sheets & tarpaulins. Personnel of D.R.S. - O.C. Lieut. Col. CORRILL + GOSSE, D.M.S. Sergt Major, other ranks 67, assisted by 25 light duty patients. Weather - fair + dry, rain with a heavy shower of rain at 8.45pm. J.F.C.	Plan of D.R.S. appendix 2.
	7/6/17	3.15AM	Zero hour.	
		2AM	Convoy of sick arrived.	
		6AM	First convoy of lightly wounded arrived.	
		9AM 11AM 2pm	Patients in D.R.S. 186. 65 wounded + "Shell shock" cases + 10 sick evacuated (2nd convoy cars of sergt. Cars & sent to hosp. there have been 1m Smiths J.F. Crumbie W. H. L. R.A.M.C.	

WAR DIARY or INTELLIGENCE SUMMARY

Army Form C. 2118

Place	Date	Hour	Summary of Events and Information	Remarks and references to Appendices
Sheet 27 N E L.18.d.3.6	7/6/17	6 p.m.	Heavy storm of rain & thunderstorm	
	"	10 p.m.	Says every appear. Everything working smoothly — all patients received are immediately on arrival, but having a bath, a change of clean underclothes & their wet clothes disinfected by "Thresh" & earning. J.F.C.	
	8/6/17	9 A.M.	Several convoys arrived during the night — Number in hospital 686 — There include 8 slightly gassed by shellos 36 suffering from more symptoms though the explosion of shells in the vicinity. Number in hospital 5.30.	
		6 p.m.	A considerable number of cases were during the day returned to duty. Transferred to B.C.S. at 6 & 7 P.M. 1 out Station. Capts Elliot & Boyle reported their return from 138 Field and 150 patients bathed during the day — Nothing delays by trucs cars of Lorlir. J.F.C.	
	9/6/17	9 A.M.	Number in hospital — 547	
		6 p.m.	Number bathed — 170. Number returned to duty 190 Number admitted 85	

J. F. Crombie
Lt. Col. R.A.M.C.

WAR DIARY or INTELLIGENCE SUMMARY

Army Form C. 2118

ORDERLY ROOM
30 JUN 1917
No. 599
130TH FIELD AMBULANCE

Place	Date	Hour	Summary of Events and Information	Remarks and references to Appendices
ShrapNE L28d36	10/6/17	9 AM	Number in hospital 507	
		Noon	Two horse Subdivisions & all the horse transport reported their arrival from 130 Field Amb. During the past three days there have been admitted 35 cases of no-enteric shell shock or shell neuroses & 18 others who have been treated. All patients have been held for complete returns up to 11.00 having been accumulated during the preceding ten days.	J.C.
	11/6/17	9 AM	Evacuations normal from SAM.	
			Patients in D.R.S. 500	
		noon	O.D.R.S. 2 tc cases sent to D.R.S.	
		7 pm	2 off + tent subdivision reported their arrival from Corps horse Dummy Station	J.C.
	12/6/17	9 AM	Patients in D.R.S. = 461.	
		10 AM	Six motor ambulances returned.	
		7.30 pm	SSM received from A.D.M.S. with orders for this field ambulance to take over school of sanitation, BOESCHEPE & field to the North of it as a divisional rest station. One tent subdivision & one horse subdivision to be left at D.R.S. HOPEAHOER until all patients of X Corps are evacuated. Move to be completed by 6 pm June 13.	O.O. 9.0 H. appendix 3 J.F.Crombie Lt Col

WAR DIARY or INTELLIGENCE SUMMARY

(Erase heading not required.)

Army Form C. 2118

Place	Date	Hour	Summary of Events and Information	Remarks and references to Appendices
Sheet 27 NE I 28.d.3.6	13/6/17	9AM	Patients in D.R.S. # 456	
		5.45pm	Headqrs in two moves to Sheet 27 S.E. R.10.a.3.3. 3 офс 1 tent subdivision + 1 bearer subdivision left at D.R.S. with no directions to gradually empty D.R.S. by 15 inst.	
		6pm	No further patients to be admitted to D.R.S.	
		6.30pm	Main body took Quarters of Corps School of Sanitation at R.10.x.33 with H.Qrs. room at 21 Rue de POPERINGHE. Nurse lines in a field N.E. of the school + A.S.C. billetted in adjacent buildings. J.L.	
		11.9AM	Orderlies equipment bell tents + tents obtained from area commandant in field to N.E. of School — cleared up field — horse lines moved from horse lines standing to + hut erected.	
		9.30AM	A.D.M.S. saw O.R. + P.O. men at O.R.S. Patients in D.R.S. 363 J.T. Bingham Lt/col R.A.M.C. O.C. 130 Field Amb.	

WAR DIARY
or
INTELLIGENCE SUMMARY

Army Form C. 2118

Place	Date	Hour	Summary of Events and Information	Remarks and references to Appendices
Sheet 27 B10 a 33	15/6/17	9 AM	Patients in D.R.S. 284 Conference with K.D.M.S. Men employed cleaning up Freyburg Camp – Kit Inspection	
	16/6/17	9 AM	Patients in D.R.S. 198. Capt Evans proceeded to 180 Bde R.F.A. as temp M.O./c.	
	17/6/17	9 AM	Patients in D.R.S. – 131	
		9.30 AM	Church parade. Capt J. Williamson proceeded to 105 Brigade as temp M.O./c.	
	18/6/17	9 AM	Patients in D.R.S. – 88 Men employed cleaning camp, washing wagons, ambulances & making garden.	
	19/6/17	9 AM	Patients in D.R.S. 68	
		3 P.M.	O.C. 97 J. Amb. arrived and took over D.R.S. all patients evacuated to small unit. Party left to clean up stores & equipment & take over furniture & J. F. Murphy R.A.M.C. W.L. Murphy R.A.M.C.	

Army Form C. 2118

WAR DIARY
or
INTELLIGENCE SUMMARY
(Erase heading not required.)

Instructions regarding War Diaries and Intelligence Summaries are contained in F.S. Regs., Part II. and the Staff Manual respectively. Title Pages will be prepared in manuscript.

ORDERLY ROOM
30 JUN 1917
No. 599
139TH FIELD AMBULANCE

Place	Date	Hour	Summary of Events and Information	Remarks and references to Appendices
Hondt?/SE R.10 a.3.3	20/6/17	9 AM	Patients in D.R.S. nil	
			All ranks returned to fundgnatro - Taking over certif'n to recover from O.C. 97" F. Amb.	
		9.5 am	Billetted in School of Sanitation, or other plan. Remainder of R.A.M.C. in tents in field as also N.T.A.S.C. A.S.C. H.T. billetted in farm buildings it being nightly likely from part of School of Sanitation used as a hospital for bad cases J.T.C. men employed cleaning ground - erecting bell tents &c	
	21/6/17	9 AM		
	22/6/17	9 AM	men employed as above - Great number being seen + when necessary detained in Corps School of Sanitation all ranks for want some other	
	23/6/17	6 am	Five marquees refitd. Small tents from Wippenhoek + erected in field - R.E. X b Corps in field field + approved plan for D.R.S. Fumigator from Amb. being erected	R Camp D.R.S. September 3

J.T. Brindley
Lt Col. R.A.M.C.

WAR DIARY or INTELLIGENCE SUMMARY

Army Form C. 2118

ORDERLY ROOM
30 JUN. 1917
No. S.O.9
134TH FIELD AMBULANCE

Place	Date	Hour	Summary of Events and Information	Remarks and references to Appendices
Sheet 27SE R.10.a.3.3	24/6/17	9 A.M.	Drainage work proceeding very slowly owing to shortage of tools. Kitchen commenced by R.E's.	J.F.C.
	25/6/17		R.A.M.C. O.O. no 20 received. All kits have been inspected during the preceding week & deficiencies made good. R.E's work proceeding slowly — ablution place commenced. All water now previously been obtained from REMY SIDING but a well in the square BOESCHEPE has now been opened & one supply water of good quality can be obtained from there.	J.F.C.
	26/6/17		Work progressing slowly owing to want of material.	J.F.C.
	27/6/17		Field Kitchen built as large kitchen hut completed — two hospital tents pitched. Are as drawing tent within as 19 men in tent.	J.F. Campbell Lt Col

WAR DIARY or INTELLIGENCE SUMMARY

Army Form C. 2118

ORDERLY ROOM — 30 JUN 1917 — 130TH FIELD AMBULANCE

Place	Date	Hour	Summary of Events and Information	Remarks and references to Appendices
Shed 27 S.E. R19.a.4.7.	18/6/17		Pack Store for 130 buffers & kits completed in form sheds up. Capt. & A.D.M.S. visited grounds. Drainage of grounds completed — J.T.C.	
	29/6/17		Lieut. Col. J. F. Chaolu R.A.M.C. proceeded on 10 days leave to Paris and Captain Holsten (RAMC (SR) assumed temporary Regt. Command. Accommodation for 150 patients arranged and temporary dining room and reception tent fitted up in the field. 100 patients admitted from 140th Field Ambulance. Captain S.S. Bosse R.A.M.C. rejoined on return from temporary duty as M.O./c 187 Brigade R.F.A. Y.F.C.	
	30/6/17		R.E. work still progressing rather slowly. Kitchen not yet begun. Officers n "R.W. Kents" H.Q. 1 Wanting to complete establishment 11. Y.F.C.	
			Distribution: Main party, Officers O.R. Water Warden 5. 164. Vitr. Worker Borstels 1. P.B. Now attached. Theta 2. Gledecaswelle 2. Leave L.32.b.6.7.Lev.27. 1. Officers 10th Durham M.O./c 2. 2. 12th Enfr. Surrey R.? 2. Total 11. 183. Y.F. Corbee Capt RAMC	

1875 Wt. W593/826 1,000,000 4/15 J.B.C. & A. A.D.S.S./Forms/C. 2118.

SECRET.   Appendix 1

139TH FIELD AMBULANCE   OPERATION ORDER

No 3.   COPY. 2

MAPS :-   SHEET 28. BELGUIM 1-20,000. N.W.
          SHEET 27. BELGUIM & FRANCE. 1-20,000. N.E.

1. NARRATIVE.

The 41st Division occuping the ST ELOI Sector have the 47th Division on their right, and the 19th Division on their left.

Two Infantry Brigades will be in the front line, the 123rd Brigade on the left, and the 124th Brigade on the right. The 122nd Infantry Brigade will be in reserve.

2. DISTRIBUTION OF MEDICAL UNITS.

(a) <u>139TH Field Ambulance</u> at WIPPENHOEK Siding L.28.d.3.b.
Accommodation to be provided for 400 cases.

(b) <u>140TH Field Ambulance</u> at N.6.a.8.8. (Prisoners of War Camp) as Corps Main Dressing Station for lightly wounded.
Accommodation for 1,000 cases in tents and huts.

(c) <u>138TH Field Ambulance</u> will evacuate the line with Headquarters at OUDERDOM, G.30.a.5.2.; A.D.S. at the Sucrerie, DICKEBUSCH, H.27.d.3.1. and Collecting Post at VOORMEZEELE.

2...

3)   The attack will take place on Zero day after several days preliminary bombardment.

Zero day will be referred to as "Z" day, and the preceding day as "Y" day.

Days after Zero, as "A", "B", "C".

4)   The attacking troops will assemble on the night previous to the attack ("Y/Z") night in their assembly areas.

5) DISTRIBUTION OF PERSONNEL.

Two bearer sub-divisions of 139th Field Ambulance (strength as per war establishment) will be in reserve at MEDICAL DUMP, OUDERDOM. They will be commanded by Capts: ELLIOTT & DOYLE, R.A.M.C. and will be in position by 6.p.m. on Y/Z night.

One tent sub-division with two Officers, Capt CROSSE I/c and Capt: Williamson, R.A.M.C. without transport, will report to Officer Commanding Corps Main Dressing Station for severely wounded at BRANDHOEK by 6.p.m. on Y/Z night.

6)   A party will be detailed, strength 1 N.C.O. & 5 men to meet a special train of freight cars (which may run from ZEVECOTEN to WIPPENHOEK, Stone Siding, when stock is available) and unload wounded and conduct them to C.C.S. at REMY SIDING.

Such transport as is required will be provided, if available.

7. TRANSPORT.

(a) Four large Motor Ambulances and two Ford Ambulance Cars in charge of Cpl: ANDERSON, A.S.C. M.T. will report to O.C. 138th Field Ambulance at A.D.S. DICKEBUSCH by 6 p.m. on Y/Z night.

Each large Ambulance will have a R.A.M.C. Orderly.

All Ambulances will have their proper compliment of Stretchers & Blankets – all spare Drivers will go with this Convoy.

Each large Ambulance will carry a petrol tin filled with drinking water and an enamel mug.

(b) Cabstand for reserve Motor Ambulances is at H 7. c. 2. 8.

Petrol & other necessities will be obtained here.

(c) Advanced Motor repair Shop is at L IDE GOED FARM G 17. c. 7. 8.

8. HORSE TRANSPORT.

6. G.S. Wagons fitted for carrying sitting wounded and 3 horse ambulance wagons in charge of a Sergeant A.S.C. H.T. will report to O.C. 138th Field Ambulance at DICKEBUSCH at 6 p.m. on Y/Z night. They will not take wagon orderlies.

Four wheeled stretchers will be sent to O.C. 138th Field Ambulance.

9. TELEPHONE ORDERLY

One trained operator will report to O.C. 138th Field Ambulance by 6 p.m. on Y/Z night.

4.

10. **A. & D. CLERK.**

One trained Clerk will report to O/c Corps Main Dressing Station for severely wounded at BRANDHOEK by 6 p.m. on Y/Z night for the purpose of extracting information and furnishing Daily State of Sick & Wounded to A.D.M.S's Office of all casualties of the 41st Division.

11. **DRESS.**

Bearer sub-divisions - skeleton order with ground-sheet.
Tent sub-division - marching order.

Officers in charge will see that all ranks are in possession of a Steel Helmet, Box Respirator, P.H. Helmet, Iron Rations, and First Field Dressing, and that water bottles are full of water.

12. The unexpired portion of the days rations and one day's rations will be carried.

13. Acknowledge.

Issued at noon 6th June 1917.

J.F. Crombie, Lt. Col. R.A.M.C
Comdg. 139th Field Ambulance.

Copy No 1. File.
" 2. War Diary.
" 3. A.D.M.S.
" 4. O.C. 138th F.A.
" 5. O.C. 140th "
" 6. ⎫
" 7. ⎬
" 8. ⎬ Spare.
" 9. ⎬
" 10. ⎭

SECRET   Appendix 3

                    ORDERLY ROOM
                    13 JUN 1917
                    No. 576
                    139TH FIELD AMBULANCE   COPY No. 2

OPERATION ORDER No. 4

by O.C. 139th Field Ambulance in accordance with
A.D.M.S. Secret No. 581

1. 139th Field Ambulance will be clear of the IInd Corps Area (WIPPENHOEK) with the exception of a holding party, by 6 p.m. June 13th.

2. 139th Field Ambulance will take over the Corps School of Sanitation, BOESCHEPE, and the large field North of it and at once proceed to make necessary arrangements for opening the Divisional Rest Station there.

3. No further sick or wounded will be admitted into the WIPPENHOEK D.R.S. after 6 p.m. 13th inst. Capts: WILLIAMSON, MULLOY & CROSSE with one tent sub-division & one bearer sub-division will be left as a holding party and will dispose of all sick & wounded of this Division, other Divisions & Xth Corps Troops by the 20th inst. gradually.

4. All marquees, tents, stores, Red Cross stores, medical & surgical equipment &c in excess of mobilization equipment will be handed over to the incoming unit, receipts being passed and copies sent to this Office.

5. A.S.C. H.T. & A.S.C. M.T. will occupy the end of the field nearest BOESCHEPE with such horse-lines & huts as may be there.

6.   The R.A.M.C. personnel will occupy the Corps School of Sanitation.

7.   Orderly Room & Quartermasters' Stores will be at Corps School of Sanitation.

8.   A & D clerks will remain at WIPPENHOEK and will render the usual returns to A.D.M.S. Office.

9.   Rations & transport for D.R.S. WIPPENHOEK will be arranged on receipt of further information.

10.   Acknowledge.

12th June 1917.
Issued at 10-30 p.m.

J. F. Crombie Lt. Col. R.A.M.C.
O.C. 139th Field Ambulance.

COPY   1. File
       2. War Diary. ✓
       3. A.D.M.S.
       4. 138th Field Ambce.
       5. 140th   "   "
       6. Capt: S.S. Crowe, R.A.M.C.
       7. Quartermaster.
       8. O.C. Incoming Unit
       9. }
       10.} Spare.

Vol 15

Confidential
War Diary
of
139th Field Ambulance
R.A.M.C.

From July 1917
To 31 August 1917

COMMITTEE FOR THE
MEDICAL HISTORY OF THE WAR
Date   10 SEP. 1917

Army Form C. 2118

139th Field Amb

WAR DIARY
or
INTELLIGENCE SUMMARY
(Erase heading not required.)

Place	Date	Hour	Summary of Events and Information	Remarks and references to Appendices
R 10 a 3.3.	1/8/17		Dispensary hut erected. Patients' ablution bench completed. 50 DRS patients and 3 RAMC personnel left for the 2nd Army Rest Camp. Captain J Williams returned from temporary duty with 10th Queen's R/S. CRE & Corps visited the camp.	
Steen 24 SE.	2/8/17		A programme of training company drill route marching etc. was commenced for the mornings. R.E. work in progress – meat store, bread store and movements could attach dugout room.	
	3/8/17		DADMS inspected the Dampierre Rest station. Patients in hospital – 60.	
	4/8/17		Meat store bread store incinerator dugout room & concrete floor on being laid on the building of an oven for the kitchen is underway yet. Captain D.G.Y. Elliott reported his return from leave.	

J.T. Cram L. Col

WAR DIARY or INTELLIGENCE SUMMARY

Army Form C. 2118

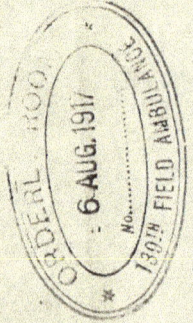

Place	Date	Hour	Summary of Events and Information	Remarks and references to Appendices
R.10 a 3.3	5/2/17		Routine work. All available men occupied in drill training. Men commenced in the kitchen.	
Shet 24 SE	6/2/17		Captain W.D.G. Murroy proceeded to 190th Brigade R.F.A. as temporary M.O./C in relief of Captain Duff on leave.	
	7/2/17		D.D.M.S. X corps completed the D.R.S.	
	8/2/17		Church Parade 9.30.	
	9/2/17		Route March for all available men. Work at present in hand in the field proceeding satisfactorily	
	10/2/17		R/Aust proved to hunt no Belgian Interpreter. Men engaged in squad Company & Stretcher drill. Sergt Pua awarded military medal	
	11/2/17		Line construction work travelling along - must safe from R.S. J.T. Dimmer. Lt Col R.A.M.C O.C. 139 Field Amb	

Army Form C. 2118.

WAR DIARY
or
INTELLIGENCE SUMMARY.
(Erase heading not required.)

ORDERLY ROOM
6 AUG 1917
130TH FIELD AMBULANCE

Place	Date	Hour	Summary of Events and Information	Remarks and references to Appendices
Sht 27 S.E. G10 a 33	10/7/17		Marching order Inspection & route march. Capt Voyle R.A.M.C reported hurt to duty from temp Hosp. 11 R.W Hunts	
	13/7/17	9 A.M	Under instructions from D.D.M.S. X Corps 80 other ranks proceeded to No 11 C.C.S at GODAERSVELDE as a working party	
	14/7/17		Capt. Williamson R.A.M.C. assumed temp. 2nd charge of C.E. Mulgan in temp G.O.C. bit. On a/m Inspected the unit — Horse Transport Divisional Rest Station & reported at Corps school Sanitation arrangements for recent into Bivouche but have found our unserviceable medical arrangements in connection with first coming Offensive Rupture received	
	16/7/17		Rupture work	
	17/7/17		Visited VOORMEZEELE, BRASSERIE & portion of front line in which this unit will be responsible during forth coming offensive	
			Belgian Interpreter posted to unit. J. T. Knight R.A.M.C	
			O.C. 130 F.A.	

T2134. Wt. W708—776. 500000. 4/15. Sir J. C. & S.

WAR DIARY
or
INTELLIGENCE SUMMARY
(Erase heading not required.)

Army Form C. 2118.

ORDERLY ROOM 6 AUG 1917 130/H FIELD AMBULANCE

Place	Date	Hour	Summary of Events and Information	Remarks and references to Appendices
Sheet 27 SE A 10 a 3.3	18/7/17		Capt. Sudley returns back from temporary duty with 190 Bde R.F.A. Visits BRASSERIE & VORMEZEELE & conferred with O.C. 6 London Field Ambulance as to improvements to be carried out at those places.	
	19/7/17		New Kitchen hut in A.D.S. in V.P. from 190.	
	20/7/17		40 men from working party at No XI C.C.S. returned. Visited BRASSERIE, VORMEZEELE & SHELLEY DUMP & inspected work at the North of VORMEZEELE.	
	21/7/17		Visited VIERSTRAAT & selected field for Transport - in the VORMEZEELE Conference at office of A.D.M.S. Church Canal & mud & inspection by C.O.	
	22/7/17		Instructions received to take over from 6 London Field amb. at VORMOZEELE to hand over D.R.S. at BOESCHEPE to 130 Field Amb. Both moves to be completed by noon July 25th	

J.F. Crumbie Lt Col

WAR DIARY or INTELLIGENCE SUMMARY

Army Form C. 2118.

Place	Date	Hour	Summary of Events and Information	Remarks and references to Appendices
Sheet 27 S.E. R.10 a.3.3	23/7/17	9am	Inspecting our return Watty dives to visited VOORMOZEELE & also huts & country to N. of Canal Bank. Sent a party of 2 off. + 30 other ranks as an advanced party to A.D.S. VOORMOZEELE.  Arranged details of taking over with O.C. 110 B.F.A.	
	24/7/17	9am	advanced party from 138th Field Amb. arrived at D.R.S.	
		10am	advanced party of 139 field amb. under Capt CORRILL left for VOORMOZEELE	
		11am	Transport left for VIERSTRAAT	
		2-15pm	Main body left in both forms a van party of 25.0 ranks under ... hun body left to R.n.Q. on to 138 F.M.B.	
		6pm	D.R.S. been very busy all day — over 240 wounded have passed through. 2nd cars arrived for duty from 130 F.Amb.	
		9pm	Considerable hostile fire in neighbourhood of A.D.S.	
	25/7/17		Many casualties admitted during the night Very wet day	
		noon	Took over from 6th London Field Amb. & handed over to 138th Field Amb.	
			J.T. Crumbie, Lt Col.	

WAR DIARY or INTELLIGENCE SUMMARY

Army Form C. 2118.

ORDERLY ROOM — 6 AUG 1917 — 139th FIELD AMBULANCE

Place	Date	Hour	Summary of Events and Information	Remarks and references to Appendices
VORMEZEELE	1917	6 p.m.	Capt Crowe & rear party report up to time. Commences to send stores to NORFOLK LODGE collecting post — this was our Tunnel Dugout at LOCK 7 Bis. Our ofondu Enemy was still shelling back area at night. Two officers & whole relieving party at BRASSERIE informed that place for walking wounded & also treating many sick & wounded.	
	26/7	8 AM	Visited NORFOLK LODGE, SHELLEY DUMP, & returned via Nahr from large motor ambs, sent by 138 F.Amb. A.D.M.S. visited BRASSERIE. Conference at HQ/ADMS.	
		5 PM	Lt. Col Craig starts to NORFOLK LODGE — Thro' C.R.S. to the R.A.P.	
		2-30	A shell struck the side of the S.R.A.P. 0 a 6.2, Zillebeke 25 N.W.4, killing No 740106 Pte OSBORNE A.G., No. 21235 Pte SQUIRES P.J. & wounding No 72069 Pte GIBSON C.W. & No. 97632 Pte SAUNDERS C.E. Pte SAUNDERS dying shortly afterwards.	
		10 p.m	137? Wounded passed through A.D.S.	

J.F. Bowyslay
Lt Col R.A.M.C.
O.C. 139 Field Amb

WAR DIARY or **INTELLIGENCE SUMMARY**
(Erase heading not required.)

Army Form C. 2118.

Instructions regarding War Diaries and Intelligence Summaries are contained in F. S. Regs., Part II. and the Staff Manual respectively. Title pages will be prepared in manuscript.

ORDERLY ROOM
6 AUG 1917
130th FIELD AMBULANCE

Place	Date	Hour	Summary of Events and Information	Remarks and references to Appendices
VORMEZEELE	27/7/17	5AM	Took Gp of Stores in C.S. wagon to NORFOLK LODGE - this O.P. B.A.P.S. now complete with all stores. Left Corp RAMC in charg at NORFOLK LODGE. Visited R.A.Ps. 2 + 3 + front line; SHELLEY DUMP Y.M.C.A. Material arrived at BRASSERIE	O 243 7 (Belgium) 28/V
		11AM	Buried three men, killed in previous day at BUS HOUSE Cemetery. Inspected roads from VOORMEZEELE to C.P.S. with Juffre. Main but had to send men to keep field free from shells. Between SHELLEY DUMP & VOORMEZEELE enough shells.	
		N/M	from 4-15 pm to 7-30 pm. Send West Kits to A.D.S. Jerry Stowe sent to SHELLEY DUMP.	
			Passed wound from BLUEE C.P. + 151 patients Evaced through A.D.S.	

J J Humphries
Lt Col RAMC

WAR DIARY
or
INTELLIGENCE SUMMARY
(Erase heading not required.)

Army Form C. 2118.

ORDERLY ROOM
6 AUG 1917
139th FIELD AMBULANCE

Place	Date	Hour	Summary of Events and Information	Remarks and references to Appendices
VORMOZEELE	28/7/17	6AM	visited Collecting Post	
		2:30pm	Visited No 3 R.A.P. & Superintended working party from 138 Field Amb. rebuilding damaged dugout.	
		7PM	VERMOOZEELE Ready Shelled till 9 pm.	
			182 patients, wounded, passed through A.D.S.	
		9pm	Work in R.A.P. no 3 completed.	
	29/7/17		heavy shell fire to C.P. & during the day.	
		7AM	visited C.P.O. & patrol sanitary fatigue.	
			Met all morning & conduction of wounded was bad.	
		2pm	Working party of 138 F. Amb. employed repairing approaches between NORFOLK BRIDGE & OESTHOEK ROAD. Nebulas - 151	
	29/7/17	7AM	Parties from 138 & 140 F. Amb. reported from 7 AM onwards	
			Visited C.P.S. – Heavy enemy commenced at 6AM & wounds got into very bad conditions. Evacuation along road west from NORFOLK LODGE very difficult	

J. T. Crombie Major
O.C. 139 F. Amb.

WAR DIARY or INTELLIGENCE SUMMARY

Army Form C. 2118.

Place	Date	Hour	Summary of Events and Information	Remarks and references to Appendices
VORMOZEELE	29/7/17		Stores being sent up by lorry to R.A.P.s. Very futile job as though BRASSERIE every day - the place is very heavily sniped, patrols fitted up for walking wounded. 134 Patients passed through A.D.S.	
	30/7/17	7 A.M.	Visited C.P.o. - Very wet all morning - mud roads almost impassable. Visited BRASSERIE & found all arrangements complete for taking wounded - met DADMS "D" Corps there.
Upon all arrangements completed & all posts occupied Capt. HODGSON, CHESNEY & TODD from 132nd went to Shiny the day & also a party of men from Subdivision from 140th Amb. VORMOZEELE heavily shelled from 5.50 to 7.30 pm - road from there to ST. ELOI rendered impassable by large shell holes on those obviated by ELZENWALLE & SHAB ROAD to C.P.S.
J.J. Burke Lt. M/O	

WAR DIARY or INTELLIGENCE SUMMARY

Army Form C. 2118.

Place	Date	Hour	Summary of Events and Information	Remarks and references to Appendices
Belgium Sheet 28 NW I.31.C.3.4	31/7/17	1 AM	Enemy camp & gas shell fire in evening through mostly howitzer gas	00h05 map
		3 AM	Intense bombardment opened to right about 4 AM	
			First walking wounded under the BRASSERIE at 6.10 AM & the first stretcher case from front line under VORMEZEELE at 7 AM.	
		7 AM	Visited BRASSERIE & found evacuation proceeding satisfactorily. Every available horse ambulance & G.S. wagon were evacuating from a walking Wounded Dump run by SHELLEY LANE & caught up the first half hour. Were able to op gate faintly with the situation.	
		10 AM	Return to evacuate from BRASSERIE area 6 am 245	
		11.30 AM	Visited SHELLEY DUMP C.P. & found it clear	
		12.5 PM	Visited NORFOLK BRIDGE C.P. – evacuated 12 patients at first. Leaving 18 there who were all evacuated by 1.30 p.m.	
		1.30 PM	Visited Walking Wounded Dump, very few coming through it but many passing overland to VOORMEZEELE. Evacuation from NORFOLK BRIDGE C.P. was by Fords which either ran direct to A.D.S. or transferred their cases to large ones at SHELLEY DUMP.	

O.C. 139 Field Amb.
J.F. Cromby Lt Col A/11 8

WAR DIARY or INTELLIGENCE SUMMARY.

Army Form C. 2118.

Place	Date	Hour	Summary of Events and Information	Remarks and references to Appendices
Belgium F 31 C 3.4	31/7/17	4 p.m	Rain fell slightly all day rendering the mud road to NORFOLK BRIDGE too very indifferent for ambulances, some cars were unable to SHELLEY DUMP by Mules Stretchers	
		6 p.m	Recovery heavy & rendered to NORFOLK BRIDGE very soft & extremely difficult for trucks to get through.	
		12 p.m	Gas shells dropped infront of trucks	
			Killed during day: 46 8218 Pte LIVOCK R.M.	
			Wounded Pte GALLAGHER S.P. 56833	
			Wounded admitted: lying officers 13, O.R. 276 P.g.m. 20	
			sitting " 11, O.R. 626 P.g.m. 11	

J.F. Crombie Lt.Col RAMC
O.C. 139 Field Amb.

27 Vol 16

Aug 1917   14Oct=38

Confidential

War Diary

139th Field Ambulance

R O Clotworthy(?)

Appendices attached:—
A. (War Summary)

from
1st August 1917

To
31st August 1917

COMMITTEE FOR THE
MEDICAL HISTORY OF THE WAR
Date   -5 NOV.1917

Army Form C. 2118.

Instructions regarding War Diaries and Intelligence Summaries are contained in F.S. Regs., Part II. and the Staff Manual respectively. Title pages will be prepared in manuscript.

Medical

WAR DIARY
or
INTELLIGENCE SUMMARY.
(Erase heading not required.)

Place	Date	Hour	Summary of Events and Information	Remarks and references to Appendices
T31 C 3.4 map ZILLEBEKE Belgium Sheet 28 N.W.	1/8/17	1AM	Proceeded to NORFOLK BRIDGE with M.T. Corporal & 1 large ambulance & 2 Fords. Runner arrived now that roads were blocked & means reaching N. BRIDGE C.P. Found on our way three evacuating & another stuck in mud, with two fords to be evacuated. 8 stretcher cases wanted for daylight to continue evacuation. All cars had now to be carried from N.B.C.P. to end of Mine road, The road too narrow & by & from embltns & Jelly holes, considerable enemy shelling of road between N.B.C.P. & SHELLEY DUMP.	
		12 non	Four ambulance with team sent up — the bad inevitable service. In the evening we have horse ambulance sent up with two horse able to keep two collecting post clear though the ones we now in a gragment with mus 2 ft deep & full of chill holes — there H. Amds evacuated to SHELLEY DUMP when cars were transferred to large motor ambulance & evacuation at A.D.S. of BRASSERIE provided satisfactory. M By & the evacuation was always kept well in hand. 7576 Cpl. SEDGELEY R.A.M.C. wounded slightly — Remain by duty. Number admitted — J.J. Humber K.Col.	

WAR DIARY
or
INTELLIGENCE SUMMARY

Army Form C. 2118.

Place	Date	Hour	Summary of Events and Information	Remarks and references to Appendices
I 31. C.3.4	1/8/17		Number admitted 6 A.M. July 31st to 6 A.M. Aug. 1st	
			BRASSERIE - Dying O.R. 1	
			" Sitting Officers 7, other ranks 460, P.O.W. 3	
Inf. ZILLEBEKE			" " 13 " 275 " 20	
			VOORMOEZEELE laying " 4 " 160 " 8 J.I.C.	
	2/8/17	6 A.M.	There have ambulances with trams working from NORFOLK BRIDGE to SHELLEY DUMP - they carried all day but evacuated all patients up to 6. They had conveyed ?? wounded and S.	
			Evacuation to B.A.C. Proven L 66665 Pte TILLIER E.F. 66752 Pte HORTON E.S.	
			74780 Pte CREIGHTON A.E. all of 139 Field amb. still wounded.	
			Number of wounded admitted 6 A.M. Aug. 1st to 6 A.M. Aug. 2nd	
			BRASSERIE Sitting Officers 5 O.R. 233 P.O.W. 3	
			" " Dying " 13 " 164 " 8	
			A.D.S. VOORMOEZEELE Dying	
			Now ambulances working all nights guns now getting worse	
			J.T. Trumbar Lt Col	

Army Form C. 2118.

WAR DIARY
or
INTELLIGENCE SUMMARY.
(Erase heading not required.)

Place	Date	Hour	Summary of Events and Information	Remarks and references to Appendices
T31 C & 4	3/17	2AM	Horse ambulance platelets & barrages near SHELLEY DUMP – when Stanley at NORFOLK BRIDGE shell slaughter man frightens the horse which bolted the two horses were not found afterwards have upset money	
		11AM	2 horses wounded by shrapnel at SHELLEY DUMP. VOORMEZEELE horses of shells till him. All wounded evac'd down today on ordinary cart & cabs, covered with mud & mostly suffering from shock	
		10AM	PTE MATTISON A.S.C. A.T. severely wounded at SHELLEY DUMP by shell. Sent via to BRASSERIE & found evacuation by motor lorries proceeding satisfactorily.	
		5 P.M.	14 wounded came in, nearly all lay at A.D.S. – not so many walking wounded apart many sick coming here. Ill lay to both places – they are suffering chiefly from exhaustion & from chilled feet due to prolonged immersion in water. They are mostly driven down to C.C.S. Magma which entrance to patrol MONMOUTH ROAD	
		6 P.M.	Visit to NORFOLK LODGE & SHELLEY DUMP. Only a few cases at former place. Horse ambulances evacuating with great difficulty owing to state of Mud Dump. J.T. Trimble, F/Lt.	

WAR DIARY
or
INTELLIGENCE SUMMARY
(Erase heading not required.)

Army Form C. 2118.

Place	Date	Hour	Summary of Events and Information	Remarks and references to Appendices
T31.C.3.6.	3/8/17	8 p.m.	Been raining steadily all day — sent another G.S. wagon to fetch more QM ROAD even to lift number of sick cases down. Capt. JODD R.A.M.C. relieved Capt. CHESNEY at SHELLEY DUMP. Took her been stationed all day up the ST ELOI ROAD to evacuate cases from R.A.P. 3 & 4. Some of the wounded admitted today have been lying in beyond ones July 31st, they were all in wonderfully good condition though their wounds were seriously infected. Wounded admitted 6 A.M. 4-8-17 to 6 A.M. wounded.	
			BRASSERIE Off R O.R. 31 P.O.W. 1	
			VOORMEZEELE Sitting " 1 " 49	
			Lying " 5 " 35 2	
	4/8/17	6 A.M.	Three horses wounded at SHELLEY DUMP	
		10 A.M.	Capt. JODD R.A.M.C. ordered to proceed to 130 Field Amb. Capt. MULLOY met to BRASSERIE for duty.	
			J.F. Crumbie Lt Col	

WAR DIARY
or
INTELLIGENCE SUMMARY.
(Erase heading not required.)

Army Form C. 2118.

Place	Date	Hour	Summary of Events and Information	Remarks and references to Appendices
I.31.c.3.4.	4/7/17	1/1 AM	Left halting from forward teams reported to BRASSERIE for duty. Item relieved by Capt. Cantrell. Running off van all day. Sent cars to NORFOLK BRIDGE where they had ordered being refused with posterior. Item ambulances with 6 horse cars now replacing these ambulances with teams. Two G.S. wagons working day & night taking walking wounded & sick from SHELLEY DUMP to BRASSERIE, one horse ambulance taking similar cases from VOORMEZEELE to BRASSERIE. A great many sick and wounded drawn chiefly early French feet. Several wounded in the way of P.O.W. came down during the day who had been wounded on July 31st — some towards were hospitals' pass parties tatters were full of traffic.	
	5/7/17	9 AM	One sunken truck ambulance car in a shell hole — the slobs has beginning damaged by Shrapnel — VOORMEZEELE heavily shelled with by high velocity naval guns.	
		3/4 AM	5 motor cars re. returned to 47th Division.	
		4/4 AM	One Ford & three driver A.S.C.T. returned to 25th Division J.F. Cranested A.D.	

T2134. Wt. W708—776. 500000. 4/15. Sir J. C. & S.

WAR DIARY
INTELLIGENCE SUMMARY
(Erase heading not required.)

Army Form C. 2118.

Place	Date	Hour	Summary of Events and Information	Remarks and references to Appendices
I 31 C 3 2	5/8/19	6 p.m.	Hundreds of milk afforting at VOORMOZEELE & the BRASSERIE. Two trench mortar aimed trays who had been wounded on July 31st, they were in quite poor condition having been in a dugout & had received food. Numbers admitted 6 A.M. 4th Aug. to 6 A.M. 5th Aug.:	
			Offr O.R. P.O.W.	
			BRASSERIE Sitting nil 36 nil	
			VOORMOZEELE " " 1 21 nil	
			" Lying " 3 18 1	
			Numbers from 6 A.M. 5th Aug. to 6 A.M. 6th Aug.:	
			BRASSERIE Sitting Offr nil O.R. 26	
			VOORMOZEELE " " 4 51	
			" Lying " 8 58	
	6/8/19	9 A.M.	Enemy in morning afternoon & taught & evening VOORMOZEELE bombarded with shrapnel for an hour.	
		10-30 A.M.	One horse subdivision 1/140 field amb. returned to H.Q. & amb. 6 horse still unfinished for ambulances between NORFOLK LODGE & SHEALEY DUMP as road is very bad. J.F. Beardsle M. Col.	

Place	Date	Hour	Summary of Events and Information	Remarks and references to Appendices
I31c3.4	6/6/17	10.30 A.M.	Hope and continuing to evacuate sitting cases from A.D.S. to BRASSERIE. Spent many visits in both places.	
		1 P.M.	Killed at FUSILIER and Pont C<u>ie</u> BARTON & HUDSON. 9 (nother) Amb. - wounded Pte JOHNSTON J. of 140 fd amb.	
		6 P.M.	B form now required for Ambulance from NORFOLK LODGE.	
		7 C. Sqn. 6.7 P.M.	Thought we had her been wounded in July 5th, they had been hurt looked after in a dugout by Autos & fed – they were sent to hospital away before owing to enemy shocking fire. An improvised bath hence has been fixed up at A.D.S. 77 hrs. has a bath & clean change of clothes today, 23 men has clean clothing.	
			Wounded admitted aug 6 6 a.m. to Aug 7 6 a.m.	
			BRASSERIE Sitting Offrs Ml OR 18, OR M w.t.	
			VOORMEZEELE " 0 " 36 " 0	
			Sgny " 2 " 65 " 6	
				J J Crowther Lt Col

WAR DIARY or INTELLIGENCE SUMMARY

Army Form C. 2118.

Place	Date	Hour	Summary of Events and Information	Remarks and references to Appendices
E31C34	7/8/17	9AM	Quiet night, got many wounded after 2AM — misty in morning, fine afterwards	
		11AM	Visited NORFOLK LODGE & SHERPEY DUMP, found everything going smoothly & few cars coming down — road very bad — 6 horses in ambulance	
		5 p.m.	Returns: Motor ambulance cars to 138 & 140 F.A. etc. Visited BRASSERIE, not many passing through. 18 men had hot bath & change. 100 pairs of socks washed. Casualties admitted 6AM Aug 7th to 6AM Aug 8th	
			Off. O.R. BRASSERIE, sitting 0 12 VOORMEZEELE, lying 1 16 sitting 0 26	
	8/8/17	9AM	Quiet night & few wounded passing through — bright sunny day again drying up rapidly. Bad shell holes in good road at NORFOLK BRIDGE. 6 horses in ambulance	
		11AM	Visited BRASSERIE from transport	
		2 p.m.	Neighbourhood of VOORMEZEELE heavily shelled by an 8" from J.F. Bunches H.B. col.	

WAR DIARY
or
INTELLIGENCE SUMMARY
(Erase heading not required.)

Army Form C. 2118.

Place	Date	Hour	Summary of Events and Information	Remarks and references to Appendices
I.31.C.3.4.	8/8/17	8 h	Raining heavy.	
		9 pm	Heavy bombardment all round on front	
		11 pm	A few heavy shells fell in VOORMEZEELE. Wounded admitted 6AM 8/8 to 6AM 9/8	
			Brown Sitting O.R. 14	
			" Lying O.R. 14	
			VOORMEZEELE "	
	9/8/17		Fine day but guns very hot & affrayer [?] Few wounded. Hun at night - hurt and withdrawn to BRASSERIE Heavy night & an enemy motor lorry left at STEENIE[?] & DUMP	
		1 pm	Run to NORFOLK BRIDGE & BRIDGE itself heavily shelled at 1 pm. Road much damaged & upward impassable	
			Pr. PASSEY KANG[?] detailed to SHELLEY DUMP	
		9 pm	NORFOLK LODGE evacuated by horse ambulance - future to meet carries on stretchers but little way along road here at Green. A.S.C. H.T. slightly wounded on here by shrapnel	

J.F.C.

WAR DIARY / INTELLIGENCE SUMMARY

Army Form C. 2118.

Place	Date	Hour	Summary of Events and Information	Remarks and references to Appendices
I 31 c 3.4	9/7		Wounded admitted 6AM 9/7 to 6AM 10/7	
			BRASSERIE Sitting O.R. 13	
			VOORMEZEELE " " 29 O.J.M. 2	
			Lying Opr. 3 " 29	
	10/7	9AM	Considerable artillery activity thro' morning but very little attention from enemy. VOORMEZEELE Shelled from 9-10 AM Hose and Stores in QRM Been NORFOLK LODGE & burst the fire — no great damage was done, managed by one I.H.E. shell. Two casualties of stretcher by hand conveyed to gate where they were put in motor ambulance engines have now had a considerable part of the day.
106th Inf Bn Tuesday quiet by — with BRASSERIE & HEADQUARTERS him of Butterworth Every from 2h Corps and car convoy sent to us to take billeting costs from KOR MOZEELE to WIPPERA, but much shelling since morning.	

J. F. Bumbes L. Col.

WAR DIARY
or
INTELLIGENCE SUMMARY.
(Erase heading not required.)

Army Form C. 2118.

Place	Date	Hour	Summary of Events and Information	Remarks and references to Appendices
ISHCSh	10/8/17		Ashmore wounded from 6am 10/8/17 to 6am 11/8/17. BRASSERIE O.R. killing 10 " " " " wounded 38 VOORMEZEELE O.R. " 1	
	11/8/17	7AM	Offr. Eqpt 5, O.R. Eqpt 31, P/M 1 Visited SHELLEY DUMP & NORFOLK BRIDGE. Forms place where latter has just crossed to Eyeg Rd remaining & lying to few metres into and all rounded about before 1/M. Shortage of transport no hand carriage to DESTHOEK ROAD, thence by Vauxhall and to SHELLEY DUMP thence by Shrapnel to VOORHOEZEELE. Rails & dumpers here not enough known to get through the three statly mud on the OESTHOEK ROAD. Engineers here busy laying a ingle track famine road to NORFOLK LODGE from OESTHOEK ROAD & also siding ned at a back transit better low was during this wet night try to take in hules strethers. Visit in the morning to see of night working would again try to Iseman. Trench and Shelley	

WAR DIARY
or
INTELLIGENCE SUMMARY
(Erase heading not required.)

Army Form C. 2118.

Place	Date	Hour	Summary of Events and Information	Remarks and references to Appendices
13¼ C.4.	10/9	11AM	Conference with A.D.M.S.	
		1pm	O.C. 13th F.d Amb. & other officers arrived to help arrangements for Trng reg. collecting stores all day from C.P.O. Taking inventories	
		6pm	Lt. R.C. Smith RAMC. & Sergt of 13th F.d Amb. went to C.P. SHELLEY DUMP	
			Lt. GASSEY returned to A.D.S.	
			Casualties admitted from 6AM 11/9/17 to 6AM 12/9/17	
			BRASSIER VC. O.R. sitting 10	
			VOORMEZEELE Offr Lying 4. O.R. 24. Lying. O.R. sitting 19	
	12/9	6AM	Capt MILLAR RAMC & party from 132 Field Amb. reported their arrival	
		7AM	Capt HARRIS RAMC & 3 Bearer Subdivisions of 13th Field Amb. reported their arrival	
			for duty. N.J. Canal past NORFOLK BRIDGE	
		8AM	20 men returned to 138 F.d Amb	
		Noon	17 men returned to the F. Amb — men returned gradually during the day.	
		2pm	Lt. GASSEY returned to 136 F.d Amb & Capt BROSSE Seconded RAMC to the F.d Amb	
		4pm	Reinforcements arrived — 20 stretchers & 50 blankets sent to NORFOLK BRIDGE	

Army Form C. 2118.

WAR DIARY
or
INTELLIGENCE SUMMARY.
(Erase heading not required.)

Place	Date	Hour	Summary of Events and Information	Remarks and references to Appendices
T31.C.3.4	12/7	5.45 p.m.	Two shells fell very close to A.D.S.	
		8 p.m.	A.D.S. pretty heavily shelled. Two telegraph wires in front of annexe cut. Lt. Graham wounded.	
		9 p.m.	Lt STRUTHERS returned to 140 Fd. Amb.	
	13/7	noon	C.O. & 134 Fd. Amb. arrived at VOORZEELE & BRASSERIE at noon. BRASSERIE, SPOILBANK & SHELLEY DUMP & JUNCTION area south of Canal to be held in line by 6 p.m. & ministries complete & receipt of Canal returned by 8 p.m.	
	midnight 13/14		136 Fd. Amb. and funeral withdrawn transmitted to at BRASSERIE & Transport Lines.	
	14/7		Ahead of funeral of 140 Fd Amb and returned to unit. C/O & 2 in hand can. returned to 140 & the same to 138 Fd Amb Ambulance of 134 Fd. And ministry to live the Fond to the evacuate.	
			O.C. SEAMAN & LAPISH & wounded this morning.	
			Very few wounds coming through us.	
			Relieved, 140 Melted 6 A.M. 12th, 138. 6 A.M. 13th.	
			Brasserie O.R. Sitting 1 - VOORMEZEELE O.R. sitting 15. Lying 17.	
			J.Y. Rumble Lt. Col.	

T2134. Wt. W708—776. 500000. 4/15. Sir J. C. & S.

WAR DIARY
or
INTELLIGENCE SUMMARY.
(Erase heading not required.)

Army Form C. 2118.

Instructions regarding War Diaries and Intelligence Summaries are contained in F. S. Regs., Part II. and the Staff Manual respectively. Title pages will be prepared in manuscript.

Place	Date	Hour	Summary of Events and Information	Remarks and references to Appendices
I31.C.3,4 Inf	14/7/17	6.30 AM	Visited SHELLEY DUMP & NORFOLK BRIDGE with O.C. 136 Fd Amb.	
ZILLEBEKE		10 AM	Advanced Party left for neighbourhood of MENEREN	
		1.30 PM	139 Fd Amb left in detachments to the environs of the day & new replaces by samlu.	
Belgium Sheet 28 NW			136 Fd Amb detachments from 136 Fd Amb Transport left. Your Bearer Subdivisions unarmed under Lieut CORRIGAN	
Sheet 27 SE (Belgian Series) X.2.b.2.3		6 PM	Handed over Collecting Post & A.D.S. to 136 Fd Amb + exchanged memory certificate	
		8 PM	Arrived at new billet 1½ miles N.N.W. of MENEREN. Several casualties in Bell tents + bivvo. Transport pulled short 1 mile N.E.	
	15/7/17	9 AM	Visited 123 Inf Brigade Hd Qu & all units ranged for collection of sick. Three G.S. Waggons left behind as prisoners lay dying to lack of N.D. horses been sent for.	
		6 PM	Your bearer Subdivisions under Lieut CORRIGAN arrived in Bivvoc.	
	16/7/17	10 AM	A.D.M.S. visited unit.	
			Lt THOMPSON reported his arrival for duty.	

J. F. Brankin
Lt. Col. R.A.M.C.

Army Form C. 2118.

WAR DIARY
or
INTELLIGENCE SUMMARY.
(Erase heading not required.)

Instructions regarding War Diaries and Intelligence Summaries are contained in F. S. Regs., Part II. and the Staff Manual respectively. Title pages will be prepared in manuscript.

Place	Date	Hour	Summary of Events and Information	Remarks and references to Appendices
Sheet 27 S.E. X 2.b.2.3 O Serre	17/9/17	9AM	Inspector of Ord. reports R.E. & Ord. knell. Airships to air park & 233 & (228 Field bye R.E. Lieut CROSSE examined arms & struck off strength Lieut H.D. Lyons Dawn Sewn men awarded the military medal. M2/149721 a/Cpl. Anderson A.G.; T/192556 Pte BENTON A.S., Th/026844 Pte NOBLE A. 9h780 Pte CREIGHTON AG; 66659 Pte STEPHENS C. 6675 Pte NEWMAN, W.A. 9h833. Pte WALDRON, J.W.	
		9PM	Enemy aeroplane bombing rain in vicinity	
	18/9/17	9AM	Inspector Ordnance & Brit branch. Instr & horse Transport inspected 1 M.D. horse buried	
		9PM	Sewn aeroplane raid in close proximity - no actual total to field very close to the camp	
	19/9/17	9AM	Ordered away to new rest day	
		10AM	Church Parade - arriving inspine - packing equipment	
		4PM	Hospital evacuator & transport (sick); 3h Ams to DRS & 3 to RCS	

J. F. Cumber Lt Col.

Army Form C. 2118.

WAR DIARY
or
INTELLIGENCE SUMMARY.
(Erase heading not required.)

Instructions regarding War Diaries and Intelligence Summaries are contained in F. S. Regs., Part II. and the Staff Manual respectively. Title pages will be prepared in manuscript.

Place	Date	Hour	Summary of Events and Information	Remarks and references to Appendices
Sheet 27 SE B Sown X 26.2.3	20/8/17	5.30 A.M.	Reveille	
		7.45 A.M.	Parade — Left billets	
		8.34 A.M.	Joined 123 Inf Brigade & marched by hand route to new billets. R.A.M.C. personnel were in full marching order with packs while the infantry had their packs carried in motor lorries	
STAPLES		1.30 P.M.	Arrived at billets between STAPLE & OXELAIRE. A number of men fell out on the march as a result of carrying full equipment in a very hot day. Two empty horse ambulances moved in rear of column & picked up the men of infantry who fell out	
"	21/8/17	9 A.M.	Evacuated a few sick to ST OMER area.	
		9.30 A.M.	Parades & march out of billets	
		10.46 A.M.	Joined Brigade & marched to training area by hand route then again carrying their packs; day very hot & roads dusty	
Sheet 36d NE F.1.C.3.5		5.10 P.M.	Arrived at new billets at HAZEBRINES. A number of men chiefly 19th MIDDLESEX (pioneer) fell out from exhaustion in hour & truth	

War Diary or Intelligence Summary

Army Form C. 2118

Place	Date	Hour	Summary of Events and Information	Remarks
Sheet 36d NE F.1.c.3.5	21/7	6 p.m.	Men accumulates in and billets as men available but having got left. Hospital arrange in an empty school. Transport parks in field in centre of village & animals on a licensed road.	
	22/7	9 A.M.	Personal move to new billets – no fresh uniform & equipment. Sanitation of billets very poor – no latrine buckets available, new latrines dug & male flyproof as soon became available. Bathing parades for swimmers in the river at 7 A.M. & p.m. all Vehicles, horses, motor lorry washed by fatigue parties at D.H.S.	
			men been commanded for P.B. men into hospital in a french Orthodox school proved by received by L. Smith, FA.	
		6.30 p.m.	Unit parade preparatory to inspection	
	24/7	11 A.M.	Inspection of 41st Division by Commander in Chief	
		2 p.m.	Working Wagons	
	25/7	9 A.M.	Kit Inspection & clothing inspection. Capt Cobham RAMC SR unwell with shitting Cross. Men of 41st Divisional Supply Column examined for classification A or B. J. Thorne Lieut 41st Col.	

WAR DIARY
or
INTELLIGENCE SUMMARY.
(Erase heading not required.)

Army Form C. 2118.

Instructions regarding War Diaries and Intelligence Summaries are contained in F. S. Regs., Part II. and the Staff Manual respectively. Title pages will be prepared in manuscript.

Place	Date	Hour	Summary of Events and Information	Remarks and references to Appendices
Sheet 36d NE F1 C,3,5	26/8/17	9.30 AM	Church Parade	
			Cpl LEWIS reported back from 2nd Army School of cookery	
			Sgt HOGGARD proceeded on leave	
	27/8/17	10/6	Capt MOLLOY RAMC reported back for duty	
		7 AM	Physical Drill — as usual every morning	
		9 AM	Route March	
		11 AM	Squad Drill	
		2 PM	Drill & fatigues interrupted by heavy rain	
	28/8/17	7 AM	Physical Drill	
		9 AM	Route March	
			Training interfered with by persistent rain all day	
	29/8/17		Capt Mulhearn RAMC reported for return from leave 28/8/17	
			Physical Drill, Route March & weather wet	
			Patients in Hospital 66	
			J.T. Crumbie Lt Col	

T2134. Wt. W708—776. 500000. 4/15. Sir J. C. & S.

Army Form C. 2118.

WAR DIARY
or
INTELLIGENCE SUMMARY.
(Erase heading not required.)

Instructions regarding War Diaries and Intelligence Summaries are contained in F. S. Regs., Part II. and the Staff Manual respectively. Title pages will be prepared in manuscript.

Place	Date	Hour	Summary of Events and Information	Remarks and references to Appendices
Sheet 36d NE 30	17/8/17	9 AM	Inspection of men entering Scentry lines. P.M. Helmets & Box Respirators. Type dull. Route march - weather presently unfavourable all equipment overhauled by sections & deficiencies noted. Patients in hospital 59.	
F1 C 3.5	31/8/17	9 AM	Route march - majordomo being examined every day. Number in hospital 57. Weather fine. Strength until	

J. F. Crumbie
Lt Col RAMC
OC 139 Field Amb.

31 AUG 1917
139 FIELD AMBULANCE

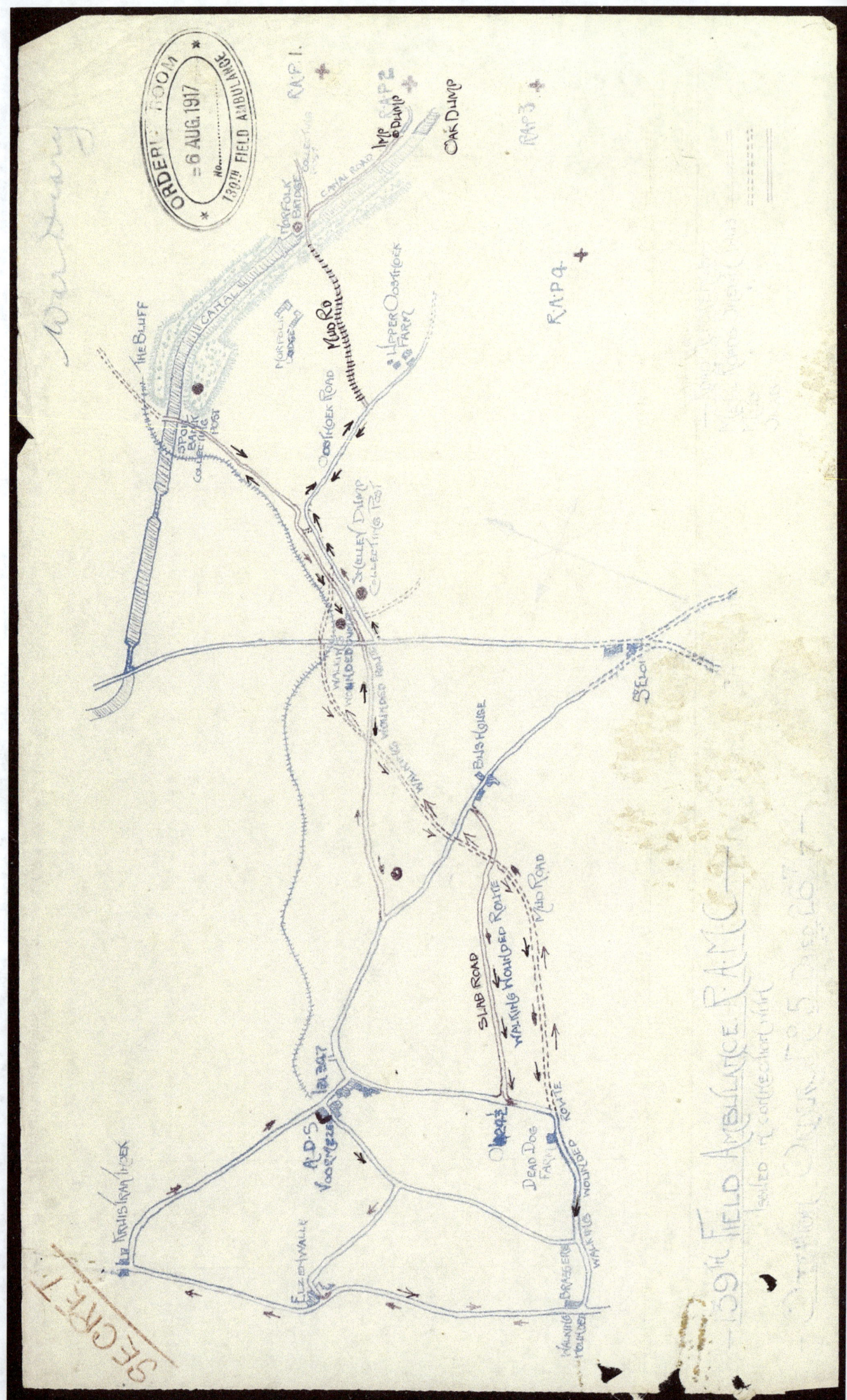

SECRET.

~~PRELIMINARY~~ OPERATION ORDER ~ No. 5.

139TH FIELD AMBULANCE.   COPY No. 1

Map References:-

ZILLEBEKE 28. N.W. 4 & N.E. 3 (part of)
28. S.E. 1.

It is hoped a special Map will be distributed later.

1 BOUNDARIES.

Northern Boundary:-

From I 36 a 86.42. - I 29 c 8.0. - I 35 a 22.75. - I 28 c 72.08. - I 33 a 64.76. - I 32 d 3.3. - thence by FRENCH TRENCH and CONVENT LANE TRENCH (both inclusive to X Corps) - thence along light railway to cross country track about N 5 a 3.8. thence along cross country track to the DICKEBUSCH - LA CLYTTE ROAD at H 33 c 0.6. (The above light railway and cross country tracks inclusive to X Corps) - thence along Southern ditch of roads DICKEBUSCH - MILLEKRUISSE - OUDERDOM and thence as at present.

Southern Boundary:-

Front line at O 11 a 2.2. - O 10 b 0.8. - DAMMESTRASSE at O 4 c 1.2. thence along the DAMMESTRASSE (inclusive to IX Corps) to DOME HOUSE thence as at present.

2. TRENCHES.

There are five main communication trenches & tracks.

N of Canal.
1. CATERPILLAR TRACK.
2. IDEAL AVENUE.
3. OAF AVENUE.

S of Canal.
1. OAK AVENUE.
2. OPTIC AVENUE.

These trenches are both for up and down traffic

2.

3. DISPOSITION MEDICAL UNITS.

(a) <u>138th Field Ambulance</u> at BOESCHEPE (Corps School of Sanitation) as a Divisional Rest Station.

(b) <u>139th Field Ambulance</u> will evacuate the line with Headquarters for transport in field near A.D.S. VIERSTRAAT.
<u>Advanced Dressing Station</u>, VOORMEZEELE.
<u>Collecting Place for Walking Wounded</u>, BRASSERIE, and <u>Collecting Posts</u> at NORFOLK BRIDGE. I 33 d.3.6.
SHELLEY DUMP   I 32 d 3.3.

(c) <u>140th Field Ambulance</u> at M 6.a.8.8. (LA CLYTTE ROAD) as <u>Main Dressing Station</u> for seriously wounded.

4. ADVANCED COLLECTING POSTS.
N of Canal A.C.P. No 1.   I.34.d.8.8
            A.C.P. No 2.   O.4.b.2½.9.
S of Canal A.C.P. No 3.   O.4.a.6.2.
            A.C.P. No 4.   O.3.d.8.6.

These are at present being used as R.A.P's, and will continue to be used as such until active operations commence, when new R.A.P's will be established a few hundred yards up the communication trenches; the <u>R.A.M.C.</u> will be <u>responsible</u> for the <u>evacuation</u> from <u>these forward</u> R.A.P's.

5. RECORDS.
Admission and Discharge Books will not be kept. Nominal Rolls will be kept at the BRASSERIE and VOORMEZEELE.

3.

6. **CASUALTY WIRES.**

(a) Battle Casualty Wires will be sent to reach A.D.M.S. Office by 6.a.m, 12 noon, and 9.p.m. for these respective periods.

They will be compiled as follows :-

A.D.M.S. 41st Division.

No .... Date ....

"Wounded admitted 6 a.m. to 12 noon a.a.a. Officers 12 a.a.a. Other ranks 120 a.a.a. Germans 3 a.a.a. Remaining in Field Ambulance Officers lying 7 Sitting 20 a.a.a. Other ranks lying 65 sitting 180 a.a.a. Germans lying 1. a.a.a.

From O.C........... Field Ambulance.

(b) The usual casualty wire affecting R.A.M.C. personnel, and A.S.C. (attached.) made up from noon to noon will be sent to 41st Division "A" and repeated to A.D.M.S. office.

(c) Casualties to medical officers will <u>immediately</u> be reported to A.D.M.S. office. Nature of casualty is to be given :- Killed, Wounded or Missing.

(d) Situation reports should be furnished as often as possible.

7. ~~TELEPHONE.~~

~~A.D.S. VOORMEZEELE to be linked up, through Headquarters 41st Division, with Main Dressing Station, CHIPPEWA. BRASSERIE may be linked up with A.D.S. VOORMEZEELE.~~

8. **ADVANCED MOTOR AMBULANCE REPAIR SHOP.**

In neighbourhood of CHIPPEWA.

4.

9. BATTLE STRAGGLERS' POSTS.
at O 2. a. 4. 6. (BUS HOUSE).
I 32. a. 4. 4.
I 33. a. 2. 3 (BRIDGE).

10. PRISONERS OF WAR.
Corps & Divisional Cage at 28 N. 3. a Central.

11. MEDICAL CONTROL POSTS.
Empty lorries will have instructions to stop if required.

12. R.E. STORES.
Divisional R.E. Dump will be at BRASSERIE.
Advanced R.E. Dumps at OAK DUMP & IMP DUMP.

13. STORES & EQUIPMENT.
EACH R.A.P.   20. Stretchers.
100. Blankets.
200. Ammonia Capsules.
One box of Medical Comforts (Cocoa, Oxo & Tinned Milk).
One box assorted Splints.
50. Shell Dressings.
One Acetylene Lamp.
Primus Stove.

EACH COLLECTING POST.
100. Stretchers.
750. Blankets.
Medical & Surgical supplies to be arranged by
Officer Commanding, 139th Field Ambulance.

A.D.S. VOORMEZEELE.
100. Stretchers
750. Blankets.
Medical & Surgical supplies to be arranged by
Officer Commanding, 139th Field Ambulance.

BRASSERIE.
250. Blankets
30. Stretchers.
Medical & Surgical supplies to be arranged
by Officer Commanding, 139th Field Ambulance.

HEADQUARTERS 139th Field Ambulance.
210. Stretchers.
   Blankets.
Reserve of all Stores.

14. CASUALTY CLEARING STATIONS.

Receiving wounded, 41st Division, will be situated at follows:—

GODWAERSVELDE.

M.A.C. is No. 11. which will evacuate from LA CLYTTE ROAD. (CHIPPEWA), and LA CLYTTE.

15. OFFICERS' EFFECTS.

All ranks will use the utmost vigilance in noting, verifying and safe-guarding all property in the possession of Sick and Wounded Officers, when first taken over and when transferred.

The N.C.O. in charge will take particular care to inspect and note whether field-glasses and revolvers are contained in their cases.

Officers admitted will be asked to name the articles of which they should be in possession, a record will be kept of the result of the enquiry, and receipts given and taken for all articles received and passed to other Units or otherwise disposed of.

When an Officer is not in a fit condition to give any information, or in case of death, a list of his effects will be taken in the presence of an Officer.

16. DISTRIBUTION R.A.M.C. PERSONNEL.

(a) RESPONSIBILITY OF COMMAND.

The Officer Commanding 139th Field Ambulance will be responsible for the Collecting Posts at NORFOLK BRIDGE and SHELLEY DUMP, the A.D.S. VOORMEZEELE and the BRASSERIE, and the evacuation from the Collecting Posts to the A.D.S & BRASSERIE.

(b) Capt: T.F. CORKILL, R.A.M.C. will be Officer in charge Forward Bearers, NORTH of the CANAL, and is responsible for the evacuation from the R.A.P's there situated to the Collecting Post NORFOLK BRIDGE. He will maintain "liason" with the Medical Officers in charge Units in that area, assist in the establishment of further R.A.P's further forward, in the event of a successful advance, and help the Regimental Medical establishments as much as possible.

He will indent on the Officer Commanding 139TH Field Ambulance for further personnel and medical & surgical supplies; if the latter cannot meet the demands the A.D.M.S. will be informed at once.

<u>Headquarters - Collecting Post, NORFOLK BRIDGE.</u>

(c) Capt: J. LA F. LAUDER, R.A.M.C. will fulfil a similar function with similar responsibilities, SOUTH of the CANAL.

<u>Headquarters - Collecting Post, SHELLEY DUMP.</u>

(d) <u>DISTRIBUTION OF PERSONNEL.</u>

O.C. 139TH Field Ambulance at VOORMEZEELE to which place all messages and reports should be sent.

(e) <u>Forward area NORTH OF CANAL.</u>

Capt CORKILL, R.A.M.C, Capt MULLOY, R.A.M.C. and three Bearer Sub-divisions of 139TH Field Ambulance.

<u>Headquarters - NORFOLK BRIDGE.</u>

(f) <u>Forward area SOUTH OF CANAL.</u>

Capt LAUDER, R.A.M.C, 1 Officer 138TH Field Ambulance, and two Bearer Sub-divisions 138TH Field Ambulance.

One Bearer-Sub-division 138TH Field Ambulance in reserve at SHELLEY DUMP to be at disposal of O¹/c Forward Bearers, SOUTH OF CANAL.

(g) <u>Collecting Post, NORFOLK BRIDGE.</u>

Capt: CROSSE, R.A.M.C.   Capt: DOYLE, R.A.M.C.
attached REV: THOMAS,   REV: A.G. GREY.

7.

(h) <u>Collecting Post - Shelley Dump.</u>
   Two Officers 138th Field Ambulance.
   <u>attached</u> Rev: McNamara, one R.C. Chaplain.

(i) <u>Walking Wounded Dump.</u>
   Major Rev: G.F. Walters.

(j) <u>A.D.S. Voormezeele.</u>
   Capt: Elliott, R.A.M.C. Capt: Williamson, R.A.M.C.
   One Officer 138th Field Ambulance.
   <u>attached</u> Rev: C.S. Dunn, Rev: F.E.A. Williams, Rev: E.S. Ellis,
   one R.C. Chaplain.

(k) <u>Brasserie.</u>
   One Officer 138th Field Ambulance.
   Lieut: Callahan, U.S.R.
   <u>attached</u> Rev: W.H. Pelham, one R.C. Chaplain.

(l) <u>Spoil Bank.</u>
   A small party R.A.M.C.
   Capt. Adamson, M.O./c H.A.G. will be stationed here.

17. <u>Scheme of Evacuation.</u>

(a) From R.A.P. No 1. by mule track or trench tramway to R.A.P. No 2, thence by Canal Road or tramway on South of Canal to Norfolk Bridge.

(b) From R.A.P's Nos 3 & 4. by hand carriage, trench tramway or wheeled stretcher to Shelley Dump.

(c) From Norfolk Bridge & Shelley Dump by Motor or horse ambulances to A.D.S. Voormezeele.

(d) <u>Walking Wounded.</u>
   These will be directed from the Collecting Posts to a Dump in the neighbourhood of Shelley Dump whence they will be evacuated by G.S. Wagons to the Brasserie.

(e) From A.D.S. Voormezeele by Divisional Motor Ambulances to M.D.S. at Chippewa.

(f) From Brasserie by Motor lorries to La Clytte

8.

18. TRANSPORT.

<u>WHEELED STRETCHERS.</u>

At disposal of O/c Forward Bearers SOUTH OF CANAL 5,
at disposal of O/c Forward Bearers NORTH OF CANAL 7.
In reserve at NORFOLK BRIDGE 5.

<u>G.S. WAGONS.</u>

Walking wounded from WALKING WOUNDED DUMP to BRASSERIE 12.
Reserve at BRASSERIE 5 and 1 pair of horses.

<u>HORSE AMBULANCES.</u>

Between A.D.S. & COLLECTING POSTS 6,
In reserve at A.D.S. 3.

<u>MOTOR AMBULANCES.</u>

Between COLLECTING POSTS & A.D.S. Fords 6, large ambulances 2.
Between A.D.S & M.D.S. large ambulances 12.

<u>TRUCKS.</u>

Officers in charge Forward Bearers will see that they are both in possession of 12 Trolleys each. Application to be made to 2nd LIEUT CARPENTER, 19TH Middlesex Regt at H.36.d.9.4, or by telegram to VOORMEZEELE DEEP DUGOUT.

<u>MOTOR CYCLISTS.</u>

Two at A.D.S. VOORMEZEELE.

19. TELEPHONE.

An R.E. Report Centre with telephone will be established at BRASSERIE, R.E. Dump, N 6 a 1.1. Medical Officer in charge BRASSERIE will keep an orderly there to send and receive messages

Similar arrangements will be in force at VOORMEZEELE Report Centre.

20. WATER.

Fifty Petrol tins will be placed at NORFOLK LODGE for distribution to R.A.P's.

Each Collecting Post will have a 20 gallon galvanized iron tank, and a few petrol tins for storing water.

A Divisional Dump of Petrol tins filled by reserve water carts will be established at NORFOLK LODGE BRIDGE, I 33.d.3.6.

2nd Lieut W.H. Saxelby, 19TH Middlesex is appointed Divisional Water Officer, telegrams :- VOORMEZEELE THE MOUND. E.W.1.

21. ARMS, PUBLIC EQUIPMENT, AMMUNITION &c.

Will be handed over if required to the nearest Stragglers' Post to re-equip Stragglers, otherwise they will be accumulated and handed over to Salvage.

22. DRESSINGS, MEDICAL COMFORTS &c.

Will be arranged by Quartermaster for each Post.

Y.M.C.A. will arrange refreshments for Walking Wounded at the BRASSERIE; M.O. i/c there will detail three orderlies to assist them; he will also detail an orderly to go with each lorry of Walking Wounded to LA CLYTTE with a nominal roll

23. SITUATION REPORTS.

Should be rendered as frequently as possible by M.O's i/c Forward Bearers, Collecting Posts & Brasserie

24. DRESS.

Stretcher Bearers, fighting Kit. Water bottles to be filled and some rations carried.
A ground sheet will be carried securely fastened to waist belt. Each bearer will be in possession of a sling, which he will retain during the operations.

Battle Positions will be taken up by 6 p.m. on "Y" Day at which time all 41st Divisional Medical arrangements will be completed.

Completion reports will be rendered by wire in accordance with above from both Officers in charge Forward Bearers & O.C. 139th Field Ambulance, the following pro-forma being used :-

    A.D.M.S,
       41st Division,
    "Arrangements completed"
        Sig: ....

Nominal Rolls from A.D.S. VOORMEZEELE & the BRASSERIE will be submitted daily to the Office of the A.D.M.S. as early as possible.

RAPID ADVANCE.

(a) In the event of a rapid advance after the capture of the GREEN LINE the Officers in charge Forward Bearers will be prepared to keep in close touch with the Advanced Collecting Posts to their rear. These Posts will be pushed forward to convenient places. The Battalion Headquarters NORTH & SOUTH of the CANAL and near CATERPILLAR TRACK might be suitable.

(b) Surplus stores will be collected at a convenient Dump near a road, a reliable man being left in charge. From there they will be removed to the CORPS DUMP at N.8.c.3.9.

25/ Acknowledge.

J.F. Crombie
Lt Col: R.A.M.C.
Comdg: 139th Field Ambulance.

26TH JULY, 1917.

Issued at 12 Noon.

COPY №	1.	War Diary.
"	" 2.	File.
"	" 3.	A.D.M.S.
"	" 4.	O.C. 138th Field Ambulance
"	" 5.	O.C. 140th Field Ambulance
"	" 6.	Capt: J. La F. Lauder.
"	" 7.	Capt: J. F. Carkill.
"	" 8.	Capt: S.S. Crosse.
"	" 9.	Capt: S.E.G. Elliott.
"	" 10.	Capt: J.S. Doyle.
"	" 11.	Capt: W.D.G. Mulloy.
"	" 12.	Capt: J. Williamson.
"	" 13.	Lieut & 2mr E. Byer.
"	" 14.	Lieut: F.F. Callaghan.
"	" 15.	Spare.
"	" 16.	"
"	" 17.	"
"	" 18.	"
"	" 19.	"
"	" 20.	"

APPENDIX "A".

The work of this Unit being chiefly that of collection and evacuation of the wounded, no more dressing of cases should be done than is absolutely necessary.

Most of the cases will have a temporary dressing applied in the R.A.P's and will be again dressed at La Clytte & Chippewa.

The greatest economy must be exercised in the use of bandages & dressings.

All cases should be carefully examined to ensure that no fractures or wounds other than the apparent one are overlooked, more especially in the case of unconscious cases.

TOURNIQUETS.

When a tourniquet is applied this should be stated on the Field Medical Card in block letters, and, if possible, a long piece of tape or gauze tied to the tourniquet.

MORPHIA.

When Morphia is given this should always be clearly stated on the Field Medical Card with time of administration; a larger amount than $\frac{1}{2}$ gr: should very seldom be given.

Abdominal cases should <u>never</u> have more than $\frac{1}{4}$ gr: and are probably better without any.

FOOD.

No case that is likely to require an anaesthetic later should have any solid food — this would include all the more seriously wounded cases

THOMAS' SPLINTS.

This should be applied to all fractures of the middle & lower third of the Femur, wounds of the Knee joint, and fractures of upper third of -

The splint should be applied over the clothes and before the wound is dressed and extension made to the suspension bar.

ANTI-TETANUS SERUM.

No A.T.S. will be given except in the case of very slight wounds where the men are returned direct to their Unit.

CLASSIFICATION & DISTRIBUTION OF WOUNDED.

All Casualties will be divided into
(1) Seriously wounded & sitting cases.
(2) Walking cases
at the Collecting Posts SPOIL BANK & SHELLEY DUMP.

Seriously wounded & sitting cases will be sent to A.D.S. VOORMEZEELE, and walking cases to the BRASSERIE.

A.D.S. VOORMEZEELE will evacuate to 140th Field Ambulance at CHIPPEWA (Prisoners of War Camp) & the BRASSERIE to 6th London Field Ambulance at LA CLYTTE.

MORIBUND CASES.

Will be evacuated from the A.D.S. VOORMEZEELE to M.D.S. CHIPPEWA.

3.

ABDOMINAL, HEAD, & CHEST CASES.

To be immediately evacuated to M.D.S. CHIPPEWA.

SELF INFLICTED WOUNDS.

Either "accidental" or "intentional", depending upon their severity either to CHIPPEWA or LA CLYTTE, care being taken that their cards are distinctly marked "S.I", and any correspondence forwarded with them.

WOUNDED PRISONERS OF WAR.

To LA CLYTTE or CHIPPEWA.

FIELD MEDICAL CARDS.

Great care must be exercised in the filling up of these cards, especially on striking out the description of the casualty which does not apply.

Cases of Nerve failure, "Shell Shock &c to be classified as Battle Casualties & as N.Y.D.N.

Gassed cases to be classified as Battle Casualties and as Gassed or N.Y.D. Gassed.

If possible a distinction should be made between cases gassed by Cloud Gas & by Gas Shells, the former being described as GASSED, C, and the latter as GASSED, S.

Morphia. Time of administration & dose should always be entered.

Name of patient & nature of wound should be in BLOCK LETTERS.

Where it is considered that a case will not require further dressing before arriving at a C.C.S. this should be indicated by a large + on the front page of Field Medical Card with approximate time of dressing.

LACHRYMATORY GAS.

The eye symptoms are best relieved by a weak solution of cocain & adrenalin, followed by castor oil. Bottles containing these & eye droppers will be supplied to Collecting Posts & A.D.S's.

CHEST WOUNDS.

Chest wounds penetrating the lungs, and having large openings admitting the free passage of blood and air, should be treated by cleansing the wound and plugging it with sterile gauze & applying rubber plaster so as to close it as nearly hermetically as possible.

SHOCK.

Injections of camphor in oil, one or two ampoules is often useful in addition to other remedies, e.g. Pituitrin, warmth &c.

J. F. Crombie
Lt. Col. R.A.M.C.
O.C. 139th Field Ambulance

Confidential

War Diary of 139 Field Ambulance
Sept 1st 1917 to Sept 30th 1917.

Volume II

COMMITTEE FOR THE
MEDICAL HISTORY OF THE WAR
Date — 8 DEC. 1917

WAR DIARY
or
INTELLIGENCE SUMMARY.
(Erase heading not required.)

Army Form C. 2118.

Place	Date	Hour	Summary of Events and Information	Remarks and references to Appendices
Shut Shed NE	1/9/17		Whole unit bathed in Divisional baths & received clean underclothing. Squad & Company Drill	
	2/9/17	9AM	Inspection Parade	
		10.15AM	Church Parade - all denominations & ranks	
		11AM	A.D.M.S. saw O.B. & O.D. men & inspected billets & hospital. Weather wet & stormy	
			66775 Pte SAUNDERS W.C. sent in convalescent camp Country Res	
	3/9/17		Weather Improved	
		9AM	Route March - Squad Drill - tent pitching - inspection	
		2PM	Company Drill - tents being returned to Q.S. Unsure how to	
		3PM	Six Aeroplane bombs fell into fields about 250 yds to N.E. of billets - no hut	
		10PM	hit except - no damage was done	
			Route March - Company Drill etc. Capt McCLAYSON to R.C. Strung	
	4/9/17		as temp M.O.C.	
			Lt Mockham returns from D.Holt. (fr. leave) J.F. Murray Lt	

WAR DIARY
or
INTELLIGENCE SUMMARY
(Erase heading not required.)

Army Form C. 2118.

Instructions regarding War Diaries and Intelligence Summaries are contained in F. S. Regs., Part II. and the Staff Manual respectively. Title pages will be prepared in manuscript.

Place	Date	Hour	Summary of Events and Information	Remarks and references to Appendices
Shot Std M S & F.3.d.3.2	5/7	9 AM	Route March – Company & Squad Drill	
	6/7	2 pm	Tent pitching Drill & pitching tents – attempts at platoon repairs where necessary	J.C.
			Capt BROSSE returns his acting from the Base	J.C.
	7/7		Route March Company & Squad Drill Equipment checks	
			Capt CARSE returns his arrival to bst from the Base	
		9.30 pm	2 NCO & 30 O.R's under Capt CARRICK NC left for working party to be attached to 233 G.R.E. at RIDGE WOOD	J.C.
	8/7	9 AM	Route March & Company Drill	
		10 AM	Conference Coy Comdrs Majors Long Capt Bromley Hele O.C. 13½ M. Inf.	J.C.

WAR DIARY
or
INTELLIGENCE SUMMARY
(Erase heading not required.)

Army Form C. 2118.

Place	Date	Hour	Summary of Events and Information	Remarks and references to Appendices
Shut 36d N F31d 8.8	9/7	10 A.M.	Recd. field on 50 men by ADMS to clearing no OB PO. at T.U. Wagons Laurispinter	
	2/n		Visited Lt Clytte Books Mais dressing station for making wounded, having moved when to take it over. Found it mostly occupied by R.Es W Dir. & R.G.H Arranged billets for transport with Area Commandant ST PAUL	
	10/7	9 A.M.	Route Marsh - Another equipment & clothing inspec.	
		2 P.M.	Transport of A.F.A. returns left for L.A CLYTTE Visited H.A CLYTTE M.D.S. North side commandant WESTOUTRE Lt. HOWARD D.S.A.R. taken in strength for the 8th inst.	J.F.C.
	11/7	10.30 A.M.	A. F. A. returns two wagons Medics. transport party left in two parties Lorries for L.A CLYTTE M.D.S.	
		noon	Handed in hospital at HALLINES to Lieut CROSSE RAMC Section Lt. CALLAHAN D.S.A.R. proceeds for duty to 69 Heavy Artillery Group Lt. THOMPSON R.A.M.C. to 32 Royal Fusiliers as Permanent M.O.G	
			J.F. Cumberley Lt. Col. RAMC	

T2134. Wt. W708-776. 500000. 4/15. Sir J. C. & S.

WAR DIARY
or
INTELLIGENCE SUMMARY.
(Erase heading not required.)

Army Form C. 2118.

Place	Date	Hour	Summary of Events and Information	Remarks and references to Appendices
LA CLYTTE	11/9/17	6 pm	Half an tin hut for M.D.S. for walking wounded + equipment church refugees into. but no receipts signed until the R.C.A & R.E. erected a building to accompany by them. Ground evacuated in Y.M.C.A. tent + transport on transport lines.	
	12/9/17	9 am	Store hut checked + runnings; inner stove trumpet in.	
		5 pm	Use shell transportation of Evaporators &c	
	13/9/17	9 am	Iron Queen hut being erected between front huts + transport lines. D.D.M.S. X Corps visited M.D.S. All stove hut collected + some stove tent erected at M.D.S. Iron Cubicle built. R.C.A. evacuated for self the transport lines.	
	14/9/17		Iron hut straw + bundles, drums shelves out, bell tents erected + transport washes. 2 Sections left Ashlines this morning by French units relief of B.D.C. 123 Inf Brigade	
		5 pm	Iron hut completed	

J.F. Murphy
M/Lt. R.A.M.C.

WAR DIARY or INTELLIGENCE SUMMARY

Army Form C. 2118.

(Erase heading not required.)

Place	Date	Hour	Summary of Events and Information	Remarks and references to Appendices
La Clytte	15/7	9AM	All tents erected - marquees drawn from R.E.M.S.	J.C.
		3PM	Gen. R. Byrne left the hutting of camp Surface by them	
	16/7	9AM	Marquees erected - officers were arranged - work commenced on	J.C.
			Marquee hut	
		2.15PM	C. Section arrived	
	17/7		Preparatory work being pushed on	
		3PM	Conference of officers of A.D.M.S.	
			R.M.C.'s Stores Drain.	
	18/7	10.30AM	R.D.G.T. R.M.C.'s & D.C.G. X Info visits Dumpf station	J.C.
		4PM	R.D.G.T. wept walking finely reported here	
			left well expects this Journal.	
			1 Sunburn Case sent to O.C. 146 Fd Amb	J.C.
	19/7	8AM	2nd Stutchin drawn from Ruilhac REMINGHELST	
		11-15	First walking wounded arrived & entered on to gang study action	
			of M.M. wounded all day	
			J.T. Buntin to be	

T2134. Wt. W708—776. 500000. 4/15. Sir J.C. & S.

WAR DIARY
or
INTELLIGENCE SUMMARY.
(Erase heading not required.)

Army Form C. 2118.

Place	Date	Hour	Summary of Events and Information	Remarks and references to Appendices
Lt Clyffe	1/8/17		Capt Nell R.A.M.C. departed to report to War Office. Capt Corless M.C. R.A.M.C. returned from leave of absence from —	
		4.15	Capt Evans R.A.M.C., 2 Steam Ambulances, 3 Horse Ambs. C.C.S. Wagons + two mules left to report to O.C. 1 H.O.F.A. Mob. at 6 p.m. at Voormezeele. Two cars and two Fords left late.	
		6.45 pm	Three Cars ATS + Ford & steadily evacuated about 150 patients to Godwaersvelde. Two clicks from 133rd Amb. reports to bearers for the purpose of entraining information number 39th Div Casualties.	
	2/8/17	9 A.M.	Steady stream of wounded all night — large ack rounds of Rural MER.	
		8.45 AM	First train load of wounded arrived at Cospa Light Railway — 89 in all. Seven trams altogether arrived at R.L.T. station up to 5.30 pm.	
			Numbers altogether 558 walking wounded.	
		10 AM	Wounded have now arriving in large numbers + continued to do so until 11 pm when the rush eased off very considerably.	
			Gents. the Cosa light railway brought arrived in both lines, being	

J.T. Cunningham M/L

Army Form C. 2118.

WAR DIARY
or
INTELLIGENCE SUMMARY.
(Erase heading not required.)

Place	Date	Hour	Summary of Events and Information	Remarks and references to Appendices
La Clytte	20/9/17		Ambulances sent large number carried out one to time by the Cafe Railway that the admission but got precedence. Every 9 men or more received between 11 & 12 noon & patients in two if every direct to the motor van then to the Buvery were admitted to the large YMCA tent. Here they rested & had refreshment when probably shifted to tent & dressed, but so it got dark — here all particulars taken. & patients not fitter — were kept on W O who entered up medical particulars & chalks & signed cards. They were next given AT SA then sent to the Buvery where transferred to by MOs — from there they filed out past a clerk who again checked the FM card, on to two marquees and thence to the evacuation tents.	
		9-30 pm	A tent sub div & 3 MOs arrived from 104th Fd Amb — they worked from 3-75 pm to 6-30 pm & undid valuable assistance.	
			The bulk of the wounded arrived between 10 AM & 4 pm — more than half had been wounded by MG bullets. A fair number of whom were less stiff though as walking, then to be conveyed into lying cases.	

J. Crommelin MC

WAR DIARY
or
INTELLIGENCE SUMMARY.
(Erase heading not required.)

Army Form C. 2118.

Place	Date	Hour	Summary of Events and Information	Remarks and references to Appendices
LA CLYTTE	30/7/17		A fair proportion of cases chiefly wounded by had also to be evacuated to "Eyres", all lying cases were evacuated to B.B.S. in M.A.C. Motor ambulances & walking cases by motor lorries to B.B.S. & D.R.S. Evacuation was somewhat slow in the afternoon as the motor lorries took so long carrying upon it was possible to commander a number of empty lorries then quickly evacuated the cases. By 7pm nearly every case had been evacuated & there were not many admissions.	
		8.30pm	all clear.	
			During the course of the day the M.D.S. was visited by Sery Gen. Laughran; the DDMS X th. Corps & by the Corps. Commander D.A. 24¢ "X" Corps.	
		7pm	Capt CORRIGAL proceeded to LARCH WOOD to O/C forward leave. The following train arrived from the battle line with walking wounded.	
			8.45 AM 87 OR - 9.20 AM 96 OR + 180 M, 9.40 AM 53 OR + 10 offr
			10-25 AM 119 OR + 10 offr, 12.15 pm 75 OR + 17 offr,
			1.50 pm 50 OR + 13 offr, 5.30 pm 35 OR + 10 offr

J.J. Cumberbirch Lt Col

WAR DIARY or INTELLIGENCE SUMMARY

Army Form C. 2118.

Place	Date	Hour	Summary of Events and Information	Remarks and references to Appendices
LA CLYTTE	20/9/17		Sunshine all day — 9pm 15 to 6 AM 16 off 1, OR 83, OR 16 wd 6AM to 12 noon off 1, OR 253 OR 16 wd, 12 noon to 9pm: off 33, OR 897, OR 16 wd 9pm to 6AM 21/9. Off 7, OR 530, OR 16 30. A very considerable number of sick and also from Bn, though 1,725 ORs Pte GROVES RAMC wounded J.C. wounded	
	21/9/17		Artillery fairly normal firing through today. O.D.M.S. visited M.D.S. in morning + O.R.S. in afternoon.	
		1-5pm	From 6 to 10 am arrivals	
		11-10pm	From 11 with 63 w. wounded arrivals. 6675 Pte NEWMAN RAMC killed. DM2/135097 Pte RAYMOND (mortally) afterwards killed 31229 Pte LLEWELLIN J RAMC, 32519 Ot. WAINWRIGHT B RAMC burned 1 N.C.O + 14 hrs sent to Capt CORRILL O/c Forward Zone Two A.S.C. M.T. reported then arrived there sent to O.C. 1 R.E. 2nd Army	
	22/9/17			
		11:30 AM	A.D.M.S. visited M.D.S. — situation kept made to have cars left with another truck	
	4pm		move to CAESTRE the following by J.C. Coyne	HAPRANG

WAR DIARY
or
INTELLIGENCE SUMMARY.
(Erase heading not required.)

Army Form C. 2118.

Place	Date	Hour	Summary of Events and Information	Remarks and references to Appendices
LA CLYTTE 23	4/17	9 AM	Handed over to a first reinforcement of 132 Field Amb. Left HELLFIRE CORNER R.A.M.C. Bearers left in charge	
		11:30 AM	Transport & personnel arrived from VORMEZEELE	
		1:50 PM	Transport left under hartley	
		4 PM	Handcarts & personnel proceeded by march route to OUDERDOM Station	
		8:5 PM	Entrained for CAESTRE	J.C.
		10:25 PM	Arrived at CAESTRE	
HONDEGHEM 4/9/17 Sheet 27 S.E. N3 & 3,7	4/17	1:5 AM	Reached billets one mile East of HONDEGHEM	
		10 AM	Infantry equipment & clothing all taken to store Fullylists gear med at intervals all day	
			WM Referred Wagons	J.C.
		9 AM	Inspection for information re.	
		1:30 PM	Transport left under Lieut. Hume & Reynolds	
		2 PM	Expo. McCloy & Bullitt(?) party left	

J.F. Bumpher Lt.Col.
O.C. 139 F.A. Aml.

WAR DIARY

Army Form C. 2118.

Place	Date	Hour	Summary of Events and Information	Remarks and references to Appendices
Sheet 27 SE	26/17		Reserville	
	6/17			
V3 b 3.7	6 AM 7th		Paraded & marched to entraining point	
			Entrained & proceeded to Pollits N of PETEGHEM	
Sheet 19	10.30pm 27/17		Arrived at Pollito	
		9.30pm	Left Pollito	
B2g c 2.2		12.30pm	Arrived at BRAY DUNES	
Sheet 19			Have all accommodation in huts save officers & billets	
D9 C 3.7			Few bell tents to be strutting tent erected. Infirmary is an accumulator	
	28/17		for sick — expect tent in J.M. plan	
			Lt. HOWARD R.S.B. proceeds to Y Corps Rest Station for duty	
			Capt REYNOLDS to be attached to M.D. to D.S.C. & Refer	
			CROSSE to England on leave	
			Open employed fitting tents — washing transport vehicles &	
			pipe Ambulance & changing up camp	
			Inspection of Regt Ambulance by Lt Col Smith J.F. transport	
			to PONTON Wounds. he Ambul to reform hybrid J. H. Long for M-Col RAMC	

WAR DIARY
of
INTELLIGENCE SUMMARY.
(Erase heading not required.)

Army Form C. 2118.

Place	Date	Hour	Summary of Events and Information	Remarks and references to Appendices
Front Line DyC3.7	29/9/17	9 AM	Inspection parade & efficiency of clothing & boots at D.H.S. Visited field cooks kitchen being rebuilt from empty tin, dugout gates &tths munching coal & watering trough for vehicles.	
	30/9/17	10 AM	Entrain in to A.D.M.S.	
		11 AM	Church Parade	
		1-30 PM	Capt Nathanson reported his arrival from 29th Division	

J. F. Crosby
Major I/C RAMC
OC 1/3/9 Field Amb

Confidential

Vol 78

War Diary.

139th Field Ambulance,

R.A.M.C.

October 1917.

VOLUME 2

Army Form C. 2118.

WAR DIARY
or
INTELLIGENCE SUMMARY.
(Erase heading not required.)

Volume 9

Place	Date	Hour	Summary of Events and Information	Remarks and references to Appendices
Shoot 19 Dy C 37	1/10/19	9 AM	Parade. Nothing by return. Remained employed fitting tents - filling spaces used by tents to ground + clearing + cleaning transport vehicles. All equipment unpacked by section + placed in field under tarps. Crews after being checked. J.T.C.	
	2/17	9 AM	Inspection order inspection. Tents being sandbagged - wagons cleaned + inspected.	
		2/pm	Marching order inspection. Sandbagging tents. J.T.C.	
	3/17	11-15 A.M.	Inspection by A.D.M.S. Inspection by A.S.C.M.T. (handing over) Stores, M.V. Belts. L.	
	4/17	9 AM	Men employed Squad lashing tents &c.	
		3 P	Received note to proceed the following day to ST. IDESBALD to arrange about billets & bringing up Personnel transport A.S.C. N.T.	

Army Form C. 2118.

WAR DIARY
or
INTELLIGENCE SUMMARY.
(Erase heading not required.)

Place	Date	Hour	Summary of Events and Information	Remarks and references to Appendices
Shut 19 DQ C3.7	5/10/17	9 AM	Advance party Capt Mulkinson RAMC & 20 O.R. left for ST IDESBALDE	
		11 AM	P.B brand by A.D.M.S. — 126 men for examination	
		2 p.m	Capt Mulloy RAMC — 12 O. Rank with 1 motor ant & 19 S. bn horse wagon left for ALECAPELLE	
		2:30 p.m	Transport left for ST IDESBALDE	
			Men only under Lt. HOWARD O.S.A.R.C. (Capt ORKNEY proceeds on leave)	
6/10/17		10 AM	Tok over from 1/3 E. Lancs at ST IDESBALDE & Attending huts B	
		10:30 AM	91st Field amb" left BRAYDONES	
		11:30 AM	Rear party 1 left BRAYDONES	
		4	Camps handed over change at ST IDESBARDE left in but condition by previous unit	
	7/10/17	4 p.m	Proceeded to ALECAPELLE to use early tree very inclement weather — blowing hard with very heavy showers rain & sleet. Men of the huven who has been accommodated in tents have be brought into an empty hut. During the day sufficient

WAR DIARY
or
INTELLIGENCE SUMMARY
(Erase heading not required.)

Army Form C. 2118

Place	Date	Hour	Summary of Events and Information	Remarks and references to Appendices
Shut II SE M10 C 7.7	7/10/17		Tents were pitched & sandbags to accumulate the whole unit. Many of them were blown down however. Sick are accumulating in one large Bernent hut. During the day truck was got with 67th 123 v/124 Brigade who are sentries along the coast from OOST DUNKIRK to BRAY DUNES. Unit employed clearing up camp & its environs.	J.C.
	8/10/17	3/m	Kit Inspection — Large number of morning sick come here every day — all cases except those returned to duty & very slight cases which are detained are sent to Corps Main Dressing Station.	J.C.
	9/10		Men employed changing position of horse lines which were flooded out during the night. Sunday wall erected to weather side. Visited AVECAPPELLE during the afternoon with A.D.M.S & selected site for new A.D.S in a cottage about 3/4 mile S.S.W of AVE CAPELLE	

J.F. Kenneshaw
W. Col. R.A.M.C

Army Form C. 2118

WAR DIARY
or
INTELLIGENCE SUMMARY
(Erase heading not required.)

Instructions regarding War Diaries and Intelligence Summaries are contained in F. S. Regs., Part II. and the Staff Manual respectively. Title Pages will be prepared in manuscript.

Place	Date	Hour	Summary of Events and Information	Remarks and references to Appendices
Shut/1 SA N10C77	10/7	9.30 A.M.	A.D.S. transfer full ambulance. Working party of 1 N.C.O. & 12 O. ranks sent to RE. Capt. Murphy at AVECAPELLE. Men employed sandbagging hospital.	JTC
	11/7		Sandbagging & EN AVECAPELLE - Sent them a working party. Visited A.D.S at AVECAPELLE of 1 N.C.O. + 13 men.	JTC
	12/7	9 AM.	Advanced party under Capt. Williamson left for Y Cafe Rousbrugge. Working party of 1 N.C.O. ranks sent to A.D.S. AVECAPELLE.	JC
		2 hr.	Party of 2 N.C.O. ranks sent to Y Cafe Rest Station under H. PORTER	LA
	13/7	9 A.M.	P. B. Bernard left for Y Cafe Rest Station	
		10 A.M.	A.D.M.S	
		11 A.M.	Transport left for Y Cafe Rest Station	

J. J. Burney
Lt Col R.A.M.C

1875 Wt. W593/826 1,000,000 4/15 J.B.C. & A. A.D.S.S./Forms/C. 2118.

Army Form C. 2118

WAR DIARY
or
INTELLIGENCE SUMMARY
(Erase heading not required.)

Place	Date	Hour	Summary of Events and Information	Remarks and references to Appendices
Sheet 11 SE M10 C.7.1	13/10/17	Noon	Visited AVECAPPELLE	
		2 p.m.	Remainder of personnel left for Y Corps Rest Station & men huts returning to hand over to 140 Field Amb.	J.F.C.
Sheet 19 D6a26	14/10/17	9 a.m.	Handed over ST IDESBALD Billets & hospital to 140 Field Amb. & took over Y(XV) Corps Rest Station from 90th Field Amb. 140 Fd. Amb. reported for duty	J.F.C.
			CAPT. ROWLAND R.A.M.C. & CAPT CLARK R.A.M.C.	
	15/10/17	Noon	XV Corps Commander & D.D.M.S. inspected Rest station	
			90th Field Ambulance left during the day.	
		6 p.m.	G.O. 2anko Canadian Railway Engineers who has been held up Nissen huts approved their work	
			Electric light in front of the huts for the first time	J.F.C.
	16/10/17		Work proceeding slowly but naturally on the two Adrian huts that were damaged by wind, two flooring officer's mess. One Nissen hut being erected & hauce & Adrian huts being sandbagged. Armstrong hut for leaths & shower ft. at M.P.R.A.M.C. J.F.Crumbie	

WAR DIARY
or
INTELLIGENCE SUMMARY
(Erase heading not required.)

Army Form C. 2118

Place	Date	Hour	Summary of Events and Information	Remarks and references to Appendices
	17/10/17	9AM	1 N.C.O & 3 men returns from Kanshan Railway Co. to build Mason Hut	
D8a26			Armstrong Hut for lmt to erected	
			Work on skin baths proceeding steadily — R.E. Officer called in afternoon with reference to this & as to scheme for drainage of camp.	
			8 cases of mild trench feet admitted	
			Sandbags being procured with no labour became available	J.T.C
	18/10/17	9AM	Armstrong Hut furnished refurnny — all Mission Huts emptied of pts to enable to began to fill them with patients from G Marquees —	
		4PM	C.R.E. & Sanitary Officer on inspection. Capt Cornish RAMC attached for duty arrived from base. Visited GROOTE KINTE & LAVECHA PELLE	
		9PM	262 patients admitted to day — 152 from the 1st Division	
			Number of patients in Hospital Officers 26. O.Ranks 957. Sick 266. Convalescents 360	

J.F Cunnybs
Lt Col. R.A.M.C

WAR DIARY or INTELLIGENCE SUMMARY

(Erase heading not required.)

Army Form C. 2118

Place	Date	Hour	Summary of Events and Information	Remarks and references to Appendices
D.8.a.2.b	19/10/17	9AM	Eleven lice in huts now occupied by patients - a row of marquees in front being struck. Sandbag proceeding slowly. Three men provided to KNOOTE X M.R.E to collect flooring for officers ward	
	20/10/17		Small linen hut being erected for the use of officers now occupying barn. JJC Cartogenne skin diseases. No 6 Admin tent completed & occupied. Tents of concealment camp being struck more much. All huts being sandbagged. Ration strength - patients - offrs 24. O.ranks 986, Unis absent camp 39². offrs 3. O.ranks 290 Total 1695	
	21/17		Skin Camp - Officers 5. Weather mainly improved - warm & sunny by day, clear & calm at night with no wind - enemy airplanes pass our camp every night. Cinema performance stopped in consequence	

J.F. Bumke M.A. RAMC
OC. 139 Field amb

WAR DIARY
or
INTELLIGENCE SUMMARY
(Erase heading not required.)

Army Form C. 2118

Place	Date	Hour	Summary of Events and Information	Remarks and references to Appendices
D8a2.6	21/10/17		Nurse Humphries struck — dangerously proceeding slowly. All leaving west & stray new patients from GROOTE KINTE. Several hostile aeroplanes from NE between 7 & 8 p.m. — bombs dropped in the vicinity of Rest Station but not near enough to do any material damage. Patients — Hospital. Offrs 25. O.ranks 970. Sick — Offrs 3. O.ranks 265. Remaining in camp. W.II. To duty 82. Admissions 135.	J.J.C.
	22/10/17		More entraining to base — marquees being struck & returned to store. All possible west & stray new detrained from C in DS at GROOTE KINTE. Patients: Admitted Offrs 81. O.ranks 691. Sick — Offrs 4. O.ranks 266. To CCS 7h. Admissions 99. Rem. camp. h 29. To duty 9h.	J.J.C.
	23/10/17		Wet & stormy all day interfering with return loads a few marquees & full tents struck. Patients — Admitted Offrs 36. O.ranks 532. Sick — Offrs 5. O.ranks 224. Rem. camp. h 66. To duty 134. Admissions 140.	J.J. Humphries RAMC Lt Col Cmdg

O.C. 136 Fd. Amb.

1875 Wt. W593/826 1,000,000 4/15 J.B.C. & A. A.D.S.S./Forms/C. 2118.

WAR DIARY
or
INTELLIGENCE SUMMARY
(Erase heading not required.)

Army Form C. 2118

Place	Date	Hour	Summary of Events and Information	Remarks and references to Appendices
Dec 26	24/10/17		Stormy day - wet & stormy at night no air raids for two nights. Patients being gradually removed from the tents few transfers to huts & no lights preventing satisfactory work. Patients Hospital Offrs. 35, O. ranks 839. Skin Offrs 5, O. ranks 201 Con. Camp. 438. To duty 119. to C.C.S. 33. admitted 114, for 2y J.F. Crombie	
	25/10/17		Very stormy all night wind rising to gale a few tents blown down but no damage to huts or tents. Officers wards for skin & fractures are occupied for first time also the tent completed Admin that all patients except some skin cases & men in convalescent camp are now accomodated in huts. Patients - Hospital Officers 30, O. ranks 802. Skin Offrs 4, O. ranks 187 Con. Camp. 381. To duty, 120 to C.C.S. 65. admitted Offrs 1, O. ranks 86 J.F. Crombie Lt Col. RAMC	

Army Form C. 2118.

WAR DIARY
or
INTELLIGENCE SUMMARY.
(Erase heading not required.)

Instructions regarding War Diaries and Intelligence Summaries are contained in F. S. Regs., Part II. and the Staff Manual respectively. Title pages will be prepared in manuscript.

Place	Date	Hour	Summary of Events and Information	Remarks and references to Appendices
D8a 7.6	26/7		Men available were employed sandbagging floor of S.S. Officers ante room. Heavy Rain. Many marquees & bell tents struck.	
			O.D.M.S. with D.A. & D.M.G. XV Corps visited Rest Station in afternoon. Patients to hospital - Offr 30. O.Ranks 801. Sick inf. Offr 5. O.Ranks 181. Evan. from p. O.Ranks 360. To C.C.S. 31. I duty Offr. 1. O.Ranks 94. Remaining fit C.	
	27/7		Sandbagging had all day & much progress made. All available canvas struck. Engines have had a considerable [?] of fire him for emergent water to pails & land. Stayed for 3 rep. into tank erected. Slab standing for both ambulance hun entrance completed.	
			Men almost full - wind high - everywhere wet at night. Patients to hospital - Offr 30. O.Ranks 77.0. Sick inf Offr 5. O.Ranks 170. Evan. from p. O.Ranks 3hb. To C.C.S. O.Ranks 49. To duty O.S. O.Ranks 86.	

J. F. [signature]
M. [signature]

WAR DIARY
or
INTELLIGENCE SUMMARY
(Erase heading not required.)

Army Form C. 2118.

Place	Date	Hour	Summary of Events and Information	Remarks and references to Appendices
D Ba 7.6	28/10/17	11 AM	OC who received to be ready to hand over Car Post Station at short notice started preparing accordingly. Two front officers been absent on photo	
		6 pm	advance parts of 27th, 7th Amb 9th Division arrived	
		8:30 pm	2 M.O + 71 O Ranks 140 7th Amb left to open their unit	
			Patients admitted. Offs 29, O Ranks 778. Sick & Inj Offs 5, O Ranks 1880	
			Evacuated. Offs 17, O Ranks to C.C.S. 42. To duty Offs 3, O Ranks 770, O Ranks 15	
			Evacuation 8/7.	
	29/10/17		hour duty of 27th Field Ambulance ended at 9 am	
			A.th & 7th 9 th am by Lorries during the day.	
			Capt. Cookill R.A.M.C. left at 3 pm to report to D.D.O.2 at Dunkirk	
		5:30 pm	Main body of Personnel left offs 2, L/A Payne	
		6 pm	Transport left G/K Payne	
		6 pm	Handed over to OC 27 Field Amb + all documents signed +	
			receipts given received	
			Patients – Amp Offs 28, O Ranks 770, Sick Offs 5, O Ranks 203	
			Evacuated to C.C.S. 42. To duty 85	
			Evacuation 273. Transport to C.C.S.	

J.F. Humphreys R.A.M.C.
OC 139 Field Amb.

Army Form C. 2118.

WAR DIARY
or
INTELLIGENCE SUMMARY.
(Erase heading not required.)

Instructions regarding War Diaries and Intelligence Summaries are contained in F. S. Regs., Part II. and the Staff Manual respectively. Title pages will be prepared in manuscript.

Place	Date	Hour	Summary of Events and Information	Remarks and references to Appendices
LA PANNE	30/9	10	Very wet all day — troops billeted in empty house — hun mud both in to clothing water subs.	
	31/9	11AM	Conference at Dr'n ADMS. Sun waistcoats issued to men — left overs of clothing intra. M&D ent to Dn — Issued comforts & extra supply of pipes moved to all hospro supplied. Rate Munday got to which to GOYS 112th RAMC J.F Munder for bot RAMC O.C 139 Field Ambulance	

T134. Wt. W708-776. 500000. 4/15. Sir J. C. & S.

Appendix 1

Fld. amb. operation order No. 11.
      with map.   (a).

Report on operations   (b).

ROUTINE ORDERS NO.227 BY LIEUT.COL.C.G.COLLET,R.A.M.C.
COMMANDING
"B" FIELD AMBULANCE,R.A.M.C.
1st September 1918.

---

915. DETAIL FOR MONDAY.

    Orderly Medical Officer - Capt.G.W.Mitchell
    Orderly Sergeant - Sergt Hill.A.
    Reveille - 6.70 a.m.
    Breakfast - 7.70 a.m.
    Parade - 9.0 a.m.
    Dinner - 12.70 p.m.
    Parade)
    Full Marching Order) - 7.70 p.m.

(Sgd) C.G.Collet,Lieut.Col.,R.A.M.C.,
Commanding "B" Field Ambulance.

A.D.M.S.
4lst. Division.

Morning report 139th. Field Ambulance 9th. August 1918

LAST NIGHTS OPERATIONS.

Our barrage put down 12 oclock midnight.
Casualties began to arrive A.D.S. 2.45 a.m.
Report from O.C. 18th. K.R.R.C. all objectives gained, easily on right, but stiff fighting on left. 6th. Division did not gain their objective by 100 yards.
Casualties mostly from left, up MILLEKRUISSE road to Left R.A.P. (Captain Christie), this was therefore reinforced in bearers etc. from main body.
(Captain Corkill is writing out an account of his part of operation which will be sent later.)

ADVANCED DRESSING STATION.
Bew
Between 4.0 and 5.0 a.m. the A.D.S. was badly congested; there was no room for dressing cases quickly. In the dressing room there is no room to dress more than two cases, and in the inner dressing room ditto. I therefore evacuated all cases to Main Dressing Station, as quickly as possible.
If any number of cases are dealt with here it is essential to have dressing done in "elephants", the two "elephants" being constructed in the back garden should be put aside for dressing rooms; the present dressing room should be used for clerks filling in cards, giving conforts and taking particulars. The remaining two elephants should be for evacuation cases thus:-

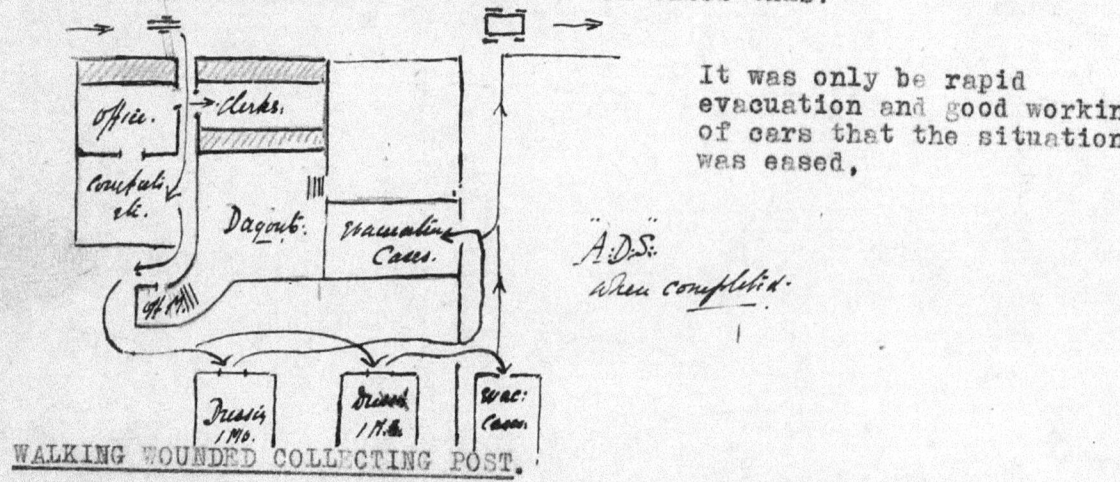

It was only be rapid evacuation and good working of cars that the situation was eased.

WALKING WOUNDED COLLECTING POST.

This worked excellently. It was a most cheery spot, with good soup, cocoa etc. and a good dressing room, but it is not big enough.
When I found walking cases were accumulating, I sent for my horse ambulances. One met a batch of 18 walking cases, juts outside RENINGHELST; the second came right up to the Walking Wounded Collecting Post at ZEVECOTEN. Thus 36 walking cases were cleared and cars eased.

LEFT FRONT REGIMENTAL AID POST

There again there was conjestion of lying cases, another elephant should be put in here and a car shelter constructed.
A shell just missed a car standing here.

CAR EVACUATION.
Worked excellently. The hun except for spasmodic shelling of RENINGHELST- POPERINGHE road, left us completely alone. Cars worked regularly up to Left. Front, R.A.P.

WOOD FARM.

On this section everything was quiet and casualties easily evacuated.

The raid on Right sector causing no trouble.

CASUALTIES.   4.30 p.m. to 9.0 a.m.

Wounded	British	Officers	3
"	"	O.Rs.	91
	American	O.Rs.	6
	German	O.Rs.	1
N.Y.D.N.	British	O.R.s	1
N.Y.D.(gassed)	"	O.R.s	1
Sick	British	O.R.s	11

Total evacuated   114

Everything was clear at 7.0 a.m. in all my medical posts. The evacuation was rapid in all parts, but there was not sufficient accommodation at A.D.S. or W.W.C.P., this is the opinion of all Medical Officers in my Unit.

WIPPENHOEK was shelled between 10.0 p.m. 2.0 a.m. last night with shrapnel and H.E. no casualties, splinters through huts and Quarter Master Stores.

Captain Corkill reports there is a possibility of some lying cases being still in front area, i.e. forward to R.A.Ps which cannot be cleared till to-night. To deal with this a bearer party and relay party is still remaining up until to-night, in close touch with temporary R.A.P. 15th.Hants and Left Front R.A.P.

Lieut.Col.R.A.M.C.
Commanding 139th.Field Ambulance

www.ingramcontent.com/pod-product-compliance
Lightning Source LLC
Chambersburg PA
CBHW080901230426
43663CB00013B/2596